VELMA WALLIS

Two Old Women

"Beautiful and moving."
—Washington Post

"Full of adventure, suspense, and obstacles overcome — an octogenarian version of Thelma and Louise triumphant."
—Kirkus Reviews

———————— ✳ ————————

Bird Girl & the Man Who Followed the Sun

"Their story will haunt the nights. A stunning book..."
—Small Press Magazine

"A wonderful read. Wallis's writing is simple yet rich..."
—West Coast Review of Books

East Third Avenue
Old Hudson Stuck
Memorial Hospital
Site
Clinic/Old
Episcopal Mission
Mission Road
Wallis
Cabin
Itchoo
Cabin
NCCO
First

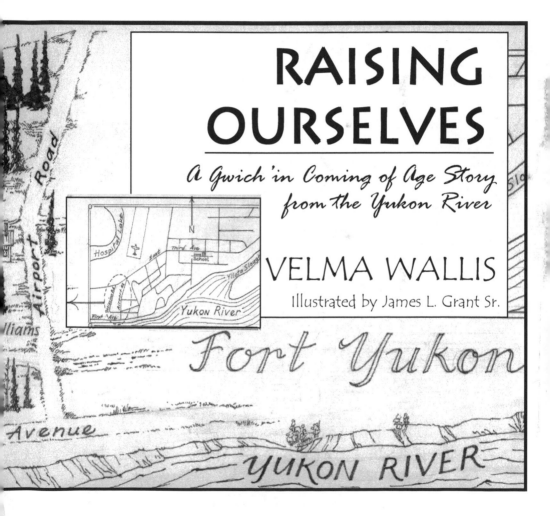

RAISING OURSELVES

A Gwich'in Coming of Age Story from the Yukon River

VELMA WALLIS

Illustrated by James L. Grant Sr.

EPICENTER PRESS
Alaska Book Adventures™

Epicenter Press is a regional press founded in Alaska whose interests include but are not limited to the arts, history, nature, and diverse cultures and lifestyles of Alaska and the Pacific Northwest. Visit us at www.EpicenterPress.com

Publisher: Kent Sturgis
Acquisitions Editor: Lael Morgan
Editor: Christine Ummel Hosler
Cover and text design: Victoria Michael, Michael Designs
Illustrations: James L. Grant, Sr.
Proofreader: Sherrill Carlson, Susan Ohrberg
Printer: Sheridan Books

Library of Congress Control Number: 2003113975
ISBN 978-0-9724944-7-2

To order copies of RAISING OURSELVES, mail $15.95 plus $6.00 for shipping to Epicenter Press, PO Box 82368, Kenmore, WA 98028. WA residents add $2.00 state sales tax. Visa, MC accepted. Order via fax (425) 481-8253, via phone to (800) 950-6663, or visit our online bookstore, www.EpicenterPress.com.

PRINTED IN THE UNITED STATES OF AMERICA

First Edition published in 2002.
Trade paperback edition published in 2003.

10 9 8 7 6

To my mother. Thank you for giving me
your blessing to write honestly.

Table of Contents

Acknowledgments

I offer my gratitude to those who aid and abet my endeavors as a writer. Thank you, Kent Sturgis. Your patience makes it easier to enter into the competitive literary world.

Thanks also to Lael Morgan, the teacher who never flinches when truth is needed. Thank you for pointing me toward Frank McCourt's Pulitzer Prize-winning book, *Angela's Ashes*; James Houston's *White Dawn*; and Harold Napoleon's *Yuuyaraq: The Way of the Human Being*.

Often after one writes a manuscript, an editor wades calmly and astutely through the myriad of unnecessary words, paragraphs, and incoherent thoughts. It is then that the light at the end of the tunnel begins to shine. You may think I am being self-deprecating, but this is my way to let others know when they have been that light. Thank you, Christine Ummel Hosler, for your steadfast editing.

Thank you to all who have written letters and met me on the street to inquire about my next book—especially you, Oscar!

Our Family Tree

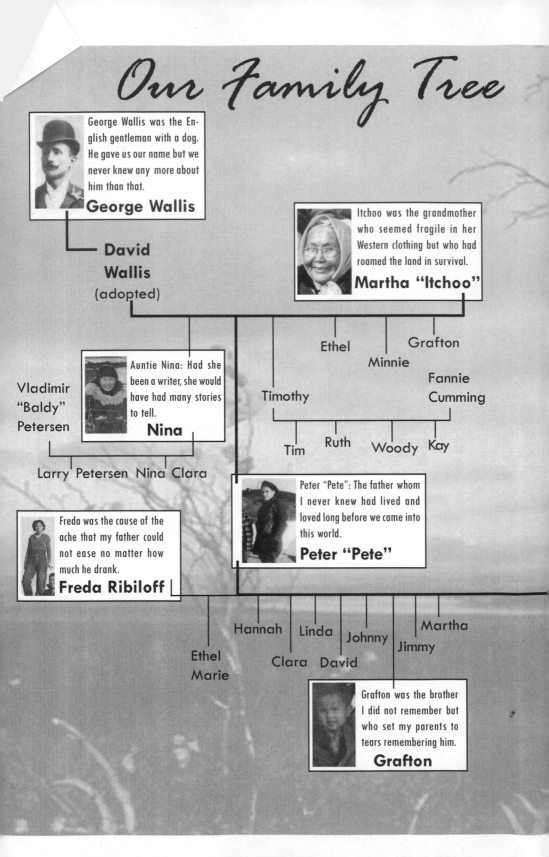

George Wallis was the English gentleman with a dog. He gave us our name but we never knew any more about him than that.
George Wallis

Itchoo was the grandmother who seemed fragile in her Western clothing but who had roamed the land in survival.
Martha "Itchoo"

David Wallis (adopted)

Ethel   Grafton
       Minnie

Auntie Nina: Had she been a writer, she would have had many stories to tell.
Nina

Vladimir "Baldy" Petersen

Timothy   Fannie Cumming

Larry Petersen Nina Clara

Tim   Ruth   Woody   Kay

Peter "Pete": The father whom I never knew had lived and loved long before we came into this world.
Peter "Pete"

Freda was the cause of the ache that my father could not ease no matter how much he drank.
Freda Ribiloff

Hannah   Linda   Martha
                    Johnny
Ethel   Clara David Jimmy
Marie

Grafton was the brother I did not remember but who set my parents to tears remembering him.
Grafton

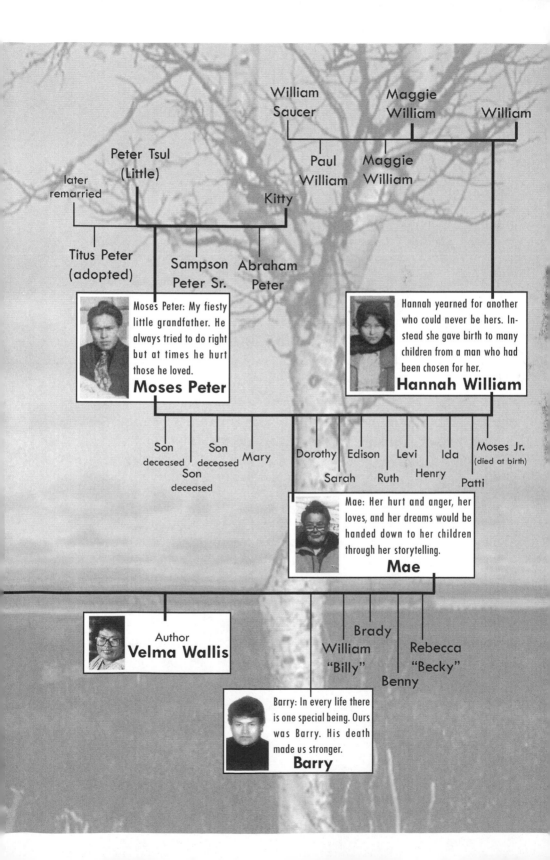

William Saucer

Maggie William

William

Peter Tsul (Little)

Paul William

Maggie William

later remarried

Kitty

Titus Peter (adopted)

Sampson Peter Sr.

Abraham Peter

Moses Peter: My fiesty little grandfather. He always tried to do right but at times he hurt those he loved.
Moses Peter

Hannah yearned for another who could never be hers. Instead she gave birth to many children from a man who had been chosen for her.
Hannah William

Son deceased

Son deceased

Mary

Dorothy

Edison

Levi

Ida

Moses Jr. (died at birth)

Son deceased

Sarah

Ruth

Henry

Patti

Mae: Her hurt and anger, her loves, and her dreams would be handed down to her children through her storytelling.
Mae

Author
Velma Wallis

Brady

William "Billy"

Rebecca "Becky"

Benny

Barry: In every life there is one special being. Ours was Barry. His death made us stronger.
Barry

Preface

It is easy to write down the legends of my ancestors, as I did in my books *Two Old Women* and *Bird Girl and the Man Who Followed the Sun*. Those characters come from an admirable past of strength and courage. They gave me inspiration in times of trial. But more important, they are stories told by elders, the keepers of oral history. Our stories testify to us as Native people of the validity of our past now that our Native lifestyle continues to be challenged by the more dominant Western culture that has overwhelmed our traditional ways.

Two events challenged me to tell my story of growing up in Fort Yukon. My brother Barry died in 1996. When he died, I did not want to tell any more stories. I wanted to live my life in silence. It seemed inevitable that, due to our upbringing, we Native people were doomed to lives overcome by our inability to cope, followed by unnatural deaths, and by unending sorrow for those we left behind.

The other event that compelled me was my reading a paper by Harold Napoleon, a successful Yupik leader from Bethel, Alaska, who was also an alcoholic. In a drunken rage, he had killed his beloved son. Later, in prison, he lamented taking the life of a loved one. In his quest to understand his own chaotic actions, he wrote a paper that thoroughly impressed me.

Harold did what most of us Native people want to do on an unconscious level but never quite achieve in our own chaotic lives. Mentally he went as far back as the first time the Western ways entered his culture. From that point on until the day he killed his son, Harold traced a sequence of unhealed trauma that each older generation visited on the younger one. Passed down from generation to generation were a whole host of behaviors that came in the guise of tradition and culture but in truth were patterns of emotional detachment, abuse, and addiction.

Our culture and people have been decimated by these self-destructive behaviors, which will only continue until we take steps to acknowledge our past honestly and to educate our young ones.

Without taking these steps, we Native people will never begin healing ourselves so that we may survive into the future.

Looking at the story of my life and that of my family makes me feel overwhelmed. How can you write about the storm if you are still in it? On a daily basis I see, hear, and participate in discouraging events that almost overshadow the positive aspects of Native life. As a child there were many times that I was happy, yet the regrettably numerous times I was unhappy were due to the alcoholism that surrounded me. Coming from an environment like this affected almost every aspect of my adult life, but now I want to shed this layer of myself and move on so that my children will have a better chance at living successfully in the fast-changing world around them.

The hardest thing for me is to tell the story of my childhood, for in the telling of my story I also must tell stories of those I love. Many times the stories about me and my loved ones are not flattering, but in order to begin healing through storytelling I must speak truthfully without intentionally dishonoring anyone. In truth, when you grow up in an environment of addiction, it is always your loved ones who cause you the greatest pain. Having said this, I will tell a story that is close to my heart and fills my soul.

CHAPTER ONE

Fort Yukon

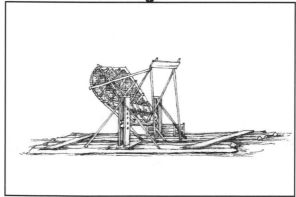

*E*arly one morning I happened to awaken as my father quietly got ready to check his fish wheel.

"If you hurry up, you can ride with me," he said, and I sprang out of bed as stealthily as possible. This was a treat I did not want to share with my sleeping siblings. My mother prepared pancakes and mush before the summer sun rose any higher. In the dawn's light, moisture sat on leaves and glistened on the grass. The flies and bees awoke with the robins and swallows, while hoards of mosquitoes hurried to seek shade from the sun's heat.

Together my father and I walked the short distance to the Yukon River, where we climbed into his eighteen-foot wooden boat. A twenty-five-horsepower Evinrude hung from the lifter. I sat on the wooden bench built into the boat, and my father perched on one of the empty five-gallon gas cans commonly used as chairs.

The village of Fort Yukon still slept at six o'clock. Only the fishermen checking their fish wheels were up and gone.

I sat still as my father pulled on the starting rope and prepared to take off. I did not want to shatter this magical event. It was not every day that I awoke early in the summer. My siblings and I usually stayed awake until eleven at night because in the summer the sun stays out twenty-four hours a day. We tried to stay up with it and usually slept until eleven or twelve the next day.

With thirteen siblings, it was not every day that I had a few precious moments alone with my father. This time was to be savored. I had to mind my outlandish tongue. My father hated us acting silly. He wanted serious children. Any sign of foolishness bought disapproval. I was the one who was always clowning. Now I held my breath and prayed to be the daughter of seriousness.

The riverboat buzzed smoothly down the Yukon. The green riverbanks were fragrant and colorfully alive with the deep purple of arctic lupine, red fireweed, yellow dandelions, and pink rose-hips. The sky was in its deepest blue, and the river reflected the earth within its smooth surface.

The boat slowly pulled up to the fish wheel, which was turned on its long axle by the strong current of the river. The two big scoops lined with chicken wire dripped with underwater growth as they were pulled out of the water. Flies had already begun to work on the huge glistening salmon, their unseeing eyes staring upward.

With great confidence and skill, my father leaned over and with his gloved hand scooped up the fish by their mouths and dropped them into a long washtub in the boat. His other hand held firmly onto the wooden box that he had built to catch any fish that fell out of the scoops.

The washtub held more than two dozen salmon when my father pushed the boat back into the flowing current and restarted the motor. As we rode back to the village, I would look back at him occasionally. His cap with the little white ribbon on the front tilted back slightly as he placidly chewed his snuff. His prematurely gray hair was trimmed into a crew cut. He was a hefty man of five-foot-six, and although I did not know it until much later, he had been a handsome man in his youth.

On our way upriver, we saw a man and woman by their fish wheel, and we waved. The summer day had begun.

We arrived back at the boat landing in front of the two-story Northern Commercial store, and we walked back to the cabin without saying a word. I had done well by keeping my tongue still, and my father was wordless in his appreciation.

My older brothers were awake by then, and they went dutifully down to the riverbank with the wooden wheelbarrow to haul fish back to the cabin. My mother patiently sharpened her knives for the long morning chore of cutting the fish to be hung on the racks. Smoke billowed out of the cache, catching rays of the sun, and flies buzzed maddeningly around my mother and the salmon.

Later that morning when my other siblings awoke, I told them of my adventure. They were envious. In a large family, one does not often feel as special as I did then. I was six.

＊ ＊ ＊

I was born in Fort Yukon, Alaska, in 1960. It was a time when John F. Kennedy and Martin Luther King Jr. were making big waves whose effects would ripple far into the future; a time when young Native men, educated in places like Mount Edgecumbe in Sitka, were beginning to rally for Native rights in Alaska.

The old Northern Commercial Co. store stood next to the Yukon River until it was moved uptown farther from the river in 1973.

Our family's two-room cabin stood a quarter-mile from the Yukon River in the heart of the hub of Fort Yukon. We were surrounded by the post office, the store, the clinic, the movie house, the restaurant, and the airport. Fort Yukon had about five hundred residents then. Our village is famed for its position eight miles above the Arctic Circle. To this day many tourists hop off small commuter planes landing in Fort Yukon and then hop right back on to return to Fairbanks, just so they can show their friends back home a certificate proving they have crossed the Arctic Circle.

Before the 1980s, every household in Fort Yukon was a tribe unto itself. Each child was surrounded by about a dozen siblings, as well as cousins, aunts, uncles, and grandparents.

At that time a state hospital was opened in Tanana, and Native women from all over Alaska went there to give birth. I was born there. Later, when I had grown up, a woman from Fort Yukon told me how, in those days, it seemed she was always climbing off the airplane from Tanana holding a newborn child just as my mother was boarding the plane with a well-rounded tummy. All they had time for was "Hello, and goodbye."

Today these women laugh heartily at those memories, but back then it was serious business. Most Fort Yukon women had from ten to thirteen children to raise.

Behind the Wallis house was a three-story log cabin that had been used as an orphanage by the Episcopal Church back in the early 1900s. Now it housed a clinic operated by the State of Alaska. One nurse was on staff, accompanied by local workers such as a janitor, a secretary, and a housekeeper. My siblings and I liked to watch all the people from Uptown pass in front of our house on their way to the clinic with their ailments.

My father was overly protective of us. We had lost a brother to a vehicle accident years before. Since we were not allowed to venture too far from the yard around our cabin, we did not know the Uptowners. We were the Downtowners. Even farther down toward the river was an old, abandoned log schoolhouse and a few people living in the old village, which we called "Ghost Town." We called the people from Ghost Town *Na'ins*, which means "brush people." The Uptowners called us *Na'ins* because we were shy around them.

In the days when Fort Yukon was constantly flooded by the river, the Red Cross came in and moved people from the Ghost Town area up to the hill where the main part of Fort Yukon now stands. The Gwich'in people back then were so grateful they decided to name that new part of town after the organization that had helped them. But because they could not speak English very well, the town got dubbed Crow Town instead of Cross Town.

Because the Uptown people were virtual strangers, we were afraid of them. Once as I stood out in our yard, listening to myself cry mournfully over a fight lost with a sibling, an old man named Sampson Peter Sr. walked by. "Hey, *trahtrayll tsul*," he said in a teasing manner, "you're always crying, every time I come down this way." I ran into the house to ask my mother what the words meant. He had called me a crybaby in our native language of Gwich'in, which I could not understand.

Beside the river stood the Northern Commercial, a descendant of the Hudson Bay fur-trading company. The NC store was our village mall. It had everything. In my time, a local man named Grafton Bergman and his wife, Hannah, managed the store for the Seattle-based company that owned it. Sometimes our parents would send us down to the store with a note, and we would come running home with boxes of crackers or cans of soup.

Just down the road was the post office. It had all these mail-boxes with little rectangular windows people would peer into to see if they had mail. We children would peek into the rectangular windows to see what was going on behind that wall of mailboxes, curious to see the bins of mail and packages. Many times the postmaster would playfully sneak up on us, and we would run squealing with glee out the door and down the steps.

Across the street was the utility building that housed the constantly droning generator that Fort Yukon had received in the 1940s, when the village began to inch toward technology. The noisy generator was an enigma, and the stern faces of the utility workers told us this place was off limits.

Other places in the neighborhood captured our curiosity. One was a log cabin we called the Cathouse that had once stored Fort Yukon's first tractors. It was directly in front of our house, and our family had beaten a narrow path past it. In the winter it was eerie to pass by the old cabin, and in the summer we younger children peeked through its windows to see what was inside.

Long before my time, a man named Nils Peterson had come to Fort Yukon and married a local woman. He brought tractors and horses into our village. I remember the remnants of this man's farm machinery lying beneath an overgrowth of thorns, willows, and grass. The Cathouse was filled with huge, oily tools hanging neatly from pegs on the walls, and many chains. Beneath the floor was a rectangular cellar for storage.

Eventually the Cathouse came to belong to Nils's son Vladimir, who was married to my father's eldest sister, Nina. Sometimes when our Uncle Vladimir parked his truck out front, we children would burst out of the woods, begging to be allowed to go into the cavernous building and look around, in awe at this strange place. Although we were fascinated by everything inside, Uncle Vladimir never encouraged us, and we knew better than to overstep the privilege of being allowed to look.

Our world was small, but our boundless curiosity made it seem larger as we explored other parts of the neighborhood that was our whole universe.

There was the house and cache that our friend Harry Carroll and his family lived in when they came from Chalkyitsik, a smaller village sixty miles north. The house they stayed in belonged to Mary Thompson, Harry's mother-in-law. A big porch built from rough-cut two-by-sixes with many spaces in between them let in outdoor light, and a dirt floor led inside.

We saw the inside of the house only during the summer, when the family stayed in Fort Yukon. There was a rectangular room with a beautiful blue cast-iron stove, which was never used because the family used only their gas stove during their stay. Three steps led to another room that held the beds. They were cream-colored hospital beds that had been auctioned off cheap from the Hudson Stuck Memorial Hospital when it had closed years before. Calico fabric hung on clothesline crisscrossing the room, creating bedrooms.

When the Carrolls were not home, we played by their little cache. It was old and had a rusted padlock. The logs of the tiny cabin fitted perfectly, and the little door had a z-shaped brace on it. At times we wondered what treasures were stored in the mysterious place and pretended that a friendly witch lived inside.

Harry Carroll's mother-in-law, Mary Thompson, lived in an even more charming cabin behind his. Mary had floral wallpaper and many pictures on her walls, mahogany-colored hutches, and delicate teacups and saucers. Her cast-iron stove was even more majestic.

Like all village grandmothers of that time, Mary Thompson kept a house that smelled like a mixture of talcum powder, dried muskrat skins, tea, and biscuits. Calico curtains portioned off two rooms toward the back of her cabin, making them into bedrooms. Big trunks were used as tables, and many shelves lined the walls, holding endless pieces of bric-a-brac. As I walked out the door onto the well-lit porch, I would see more shelves holding colorful cans, boxes, and bags tantalizing my imagination.

Our other summer friends were three children who also came from Chalkyitsik. Their father was named Charlie but most people called him by his nickname, Bunky. He had a beautiful wife with a soft, whispery voice and the children—two girls and a boy—were mischievous and fun. From June to August they lived in the two-room log cabin next door.

Both Charlie and Harry were from Fort Yukon. They had adopted Chalkyitsik as their own village and trapped the upper parts of the land. In the summer, they came to Fort Yukon to fish or to fight fires. Later, Charlie would become station manager for the Bureau of Land Management.

Mary Thompson's mother, Laura, was my grandfather David Wallis's sister. Mary was an ageless soul, one of those individuals who could get along with people of any generation. My brothers and sisters and I loved to visit her and watch her knit socks and gloves as she smoked cigarettes and told us stories. She always offered us snacks of crackers, raisins, and dry moose meat. Then at the end of summer she, too, would pack up all her things, board up her house, and go back to Chalkyitsik.

We were sorry to see our neighbors go, but we knew that the following year, after school was out, we would see their fathers and mothers unpacking all manner of possessions out of their big wooden boats with the outboard motors. Then we would know that summer had begun.

During the long, cold winter, our closest friends were Ma and Pa Williams. "Pa," or Paul, was my father's friend; Margaret ("Ma") was like Mary Thompson—she tolerated us young ones. She always had a big stash of comic books which all of us neighbor children would borrow. Sometimes we forgot to return them. Ma would get upset with us, but the next time we showed up at her door she let us borrow more.

Back then, adults were reading *True Detective* and *Romance* magazines, and we children read the comic series. Most of the adults read because there was no television and our only radio was a rebroadcast from Elmendorf Air Force Base outside of Anchorage.

My father devoured Westerns. When he read a good book, he would persuade my mother to read it, and then we would read it. Once he read a book by Louis L' Amour about two children in pioneer times who survived seemingly insurmountable odds by using the skills their father had ingrained in them. This book impressed my father because it resembled our traditional stories about strength and courage, so he recommended we all read it. I was eight at that time, and that was my first chapter book, written by an author most of us Alaskan readers respected for his accurately researched versions of the American West and its people.

Hudson Stuck Hospital and mission in the old village.

Our life as children in Fort Yukon moved as slowly and steadily as the seasons. We knew winter would bring school, rabbit snaring, sledding, and hauling in wood. In the spring we expected our muskrat tails cooked on top of the woodstove, and our beaver meat boiling in big pots, enough to feed the whole family. In the summer we knew that we would stay up late playing with our neighborhood friends. And when fall came, we would do the same things we had done the previous year. My father hauled in wood and killed a moose, and my older brothers cut the dried grass we call goose grass from along the lakes to serve as bedding for our sled dogs.

Our existence as Native people living in villages was quiet, and except for the occasional outburst of excitement, we were languid as the smoke that drifted out of our stovepipes.

CHAPTER TWO

Itchoo

*W*e were the Wallis family. Our history was short and yet long. My grandmother was named Martha, and when she married David Wallis our story began.

As children we called Grandmother Martha "Itchoo." The Gwich'in word is actually pronounced "Sitchoo," but we Wallis children were never able to speak our language properly, so we addressed our grandmother as "Itchoo."

Itchoo was always an enigma. She didn't speak fluent English, and her values differed greatly from ours. To us she was simply an odd little grandmother who dominated the lives of the adults around us. She intimidated us younger ones with her blue glass eye and Gwich'in tongue. She seemed like a foreigner to me.

But according to my mother, Itchoo was an ordinary Native woman. She did what most women could do back then—trap, hunt, and basically be a outdoorswoman. Before the white people came, the Gwich'in people lived meager lives. Their existence depended on the animals that roamed the land. The Gwich'in needed meat, clothing, and tools; animals such as the moose provided all these. This lifestyle had been in existence for thousands of years, and the Gwich'in and their counterparts throughout North America had been made tough as leather by what they had to endure, living only by their skills and their wits.

Itchoo told of the time of starvation she remembered from her childhood. The people of the harsh Arctic land often were endangered by a scarcity of fish or moose or some other animals on which they depended. When this happened, the Gwich'in people struggled fiercely to survive or they perished.

These people followed strict rules. Hunters were fed before the women and children, because the hunters had the muscle and the skill to bring in more meat. Everyone had certain tasks to perform. Women did the cooking, sewing, tanning, butchering the animals, and drying the meat, and aside from all that, the raising of the children. All this they did without complaint, for they were as tough as men. Everyone knew his or her role in the cause of group survival.

Back then, the sensible thing for a family to do was to travel as part of a larger group, which made survival more probable. But somehow Itchoo's family was traveling alone when a time of starvation came.

One by one the members of Itchoo's family died of hunger as she watched helplessly. Finally only she and her aunt were left. Their hopes of survival were fast diminishing along with their energy.

Then, by some stroke of luck, Itchoo's aunt found a dead lynx. There was no way of telling why the lynx was dead, but the two starving women cast aside all caution in their desperation for food.

Itchoo and her aunt survived on the lynx meat until they had the good fortune to meet a larger group of roaming Gwich'in. A man named Shanatti led the group. Shanatti was spoken of with great admiration by the people of long ago. They said he was a savage fighter, greatly admired, yet he was also a kind man when the situation warranted it.

According to Itchoo, Shanatti adopted her and her aunt. It was customary for a chief to take orphans and widows under his wing until someone else could marry or otherwise provide for them. They worked hard and earned his respect.

When white traders first met Shanatti, he had twenty-one women under his care. The traders saw this as wrong, assuming that these women were all his wives. They eyed the Gwich'in suspiciously.

Thus Itchoo was introduced to the western culture. My grandmother told my mother of a time when she traded her mooseskin clothing for a pretty calico dress. The traders were businessmen who wanted beaver pelts and the furs of foxes, lynxes, and wolves. When Itchoo returned to the traders days later to complain that the light fabric had been torn by a thorn, she was taught to mend the cloth with thread and needle. By accepting these trade goods—calico cloth, beads, needle and thread—my grandmother accepted a whole new way of life without any real grasp of what was happening. Itchoo was an eager customer, and in her lifetime she was to enjoy all the new culture had to offer.

✳ ✳ ✳

In time the small, roughly hewn fort by the confluence of the Yukon and Porcupine rivers became a town of trade and commerce. After the traders arrived the church people moved in, and the Gwich'in were introduced to Christianity.

Grandmother Martha "Itchoo" and my half-sister Ethel Wallis.

Itchoo believed in what is sometimes called shamanism. This belief system acknowledges the spirit within everything. It teaches that as humans we cannot be arrogant, for we are no more and no less important than the many other aspects of nature. As a result of these beliefs, the Gwich'in were able to live in harmony with Mother Earth.

When Christianity came into my ancestors' lives, it spoke of one God and brought a whole different set of rules. When the missionaries preached Hell and brimstone, the Gwich'in did a quick about-face and accepted the white man's version of religion although they already believed in a higher power. They learned the white man's rituals. No one wanted to burn in an eternal lake of fire.

As I grew up, two belief systems existed in Fort Yukon. In the open we attended either the Episcopal church or the Assembly of God church. My father, however, spoke of being a heathen. I think he was called a heathen so many times that it became a religion to him, and some of us followed his example. My mother, on the other hand, went along. The only time she disagreed with the Christian church was when an Episcopal priest told her and my father not to have any more children. Embarrassed and insulted, she moved to the Assembly of God church until that particular priest left town.

Other beliefs were whispered among the older people. My mother had a medicine bag hanging in the back porch. She forbade us to go near the thing, which, of course, made us more curious. She seemed to fear the power that the medicine man had had. In the end, to relieve her own fears, she burned the bag before any of us could play with it. How she had come to possess that bag is unknown to me. Like the other adults, she only whispered about such things, and children were not to know.

In public, the old beliefs were described not just as something of the past but also as something evil. We were discouraged from asking questions, but we heard and saw what the adults tried to hide from us. Their age-old beliefs shone through their resolve not to let us see.

Even today, I witness Gwich'in people wanting to rediscover their traditional beliefs, but they cannot pinpoint exactly what it was they once believed. Christianity has overridden our culture to such an extent that today Shamanism is only spoken about in wariness.

My father put a stop to my going to church when I was young. The preacher's wife had told me about the devil and the apocalypse, and I came running home in tears, pleading with everyone in the house to get saved before all this happened. Later I suffered from nightmares and worry. With a great frown upon his face, my father forbade me to go to that church. But when the preacher's wife promised us we would receive a gift at Christmas, I attended Sunday school without my father knowing. Christmas morning I was unable to make it to the final service and had to go to the preacher's house later that day to get my gift. His wife was upset with me for not going to church and would not give me my reward. I was a stubborn, greedy child, and I stood by her door for almost three hours until she finally relented and handed me the gift. I grabbed it and was out the door, tearing at the wrappings and discarding the pretty paper along the street in my haste to see the reward for my churchgoing that year. It was a pretty brush, comb, and mirror set. I had to hide it, though, for I remembered that my father had told me never to go near that church again.

When it came to the Episcopal church, we attended out of loyalty but we never could understand the rituals or the preaching. After my father's death, my sister Becky and I heard two teachers whispering how they detested drinking from the same communion cup as the dirty Indians. That was the last time we stepped inside a church. To us, religion is a private thing.

Life had been different in my grandmother's time. She eagerly embraced everything new, from material goods to belief systems.

People like Itchoo were taken in by the church and christened. The missionaries chose names from the Bible. My grandmother was named Martha. She was trained to help the preacher and other missionaries who had come to help build a church and start a mission. The women sewed and tanned for the preachers, while the men provided wood, water, and food. Later, the church would recruit local men to become preachers. For now, the Gwich'in men were allowed to become lay readers.

Martha became involved with the Episcopal Church, which was becoming the focal point in Gwich'in life. More people found themselves drawn to the church and to Fort Yukon. Their nomadic way of life was coming to an end.

Eventually it was arranged that Martha would marry a man named David Wallis. Back then, women hardly protested when well-meaning elders matched them up with a potential spouse.

David Wallis had come from Canada. There were two stories floating around about my grandfather. According to one story, a beautiful woman married a man who desired her, but he could not give her children, so he hired a Frenchman to do the job. The wife became resentful toward both men, and in time she took their lives with a pistol, then disappeared. The other story suggests that the Frenchman became too attached to his job and ran away with the wife; the husband followed them and disappeared as well. Both stories have the same ending—my grandfather David and his siblings became orphans. The church divided the children out to different families, and each of the siblings ended up with a different last name.

An English preacher named George Wallis adopted David and gave him the surname Wallis. After they reached adulthood, David and his siblings came to Alaska. Why they came has never been clear.

We didn't know much about George Wallis, an English preacher, left, who adopted my grandfather, David Wallis.

Perhaps it was to find their mother, who they suspected had fled in that direction. Or, if you believe the other story, they went in search of their father, who had chased after his wife and the Frenchman.

David and his siblings traveled from Canada over the mountains beyond Chalkyitsik. There along the path they ran into a woman named Marshus, and the brother with the last name Horace married her. In time the other siblings found spouses as well.

Martha became David's wife. He was a lay reader for the church, a respected position that also put Itchoo in a different light in people's eyes.

By today's standards Martha was a liberated woman. She had tasted freedom and enjoyed it, so when she married David and was expected to become a docile wife, the role came hard to her. But she did her best.

David also did his best—to all outward appearances. He was a handsome man; his mother had been tall, and either from her husband or from the Frenchman, David had inherited a stately look. Despite his role in the church and his status as a married man, he could not resist having affairs.

Apparently Martha began not to mind after a while. She and David realized theirs was not an undying love, so they handled the rest of their marriage as sensibly as possible. They raised their children together, but behind the scenes they did as they pleased.

Once as David drank with a bunch of cronies, he noticed Martha sewing contentedly. It aggravated him to no end that she gave the appearance of being an obedient wife when he knew otherwise.

"So, you think you're too good to drink with us, huh?" David tried to goad Martha into revealing her quick temper.

The other men had heard rumors about this couple's secret marital discord, and they remained quiet, not wanting to be a part of an argument.

Martha took her thimble and handed it to David, saying, "Fill it to the rim."

That broke the tension, and the men, including David, broke into hearty laughter as Martha drank her thimbleful of whiskey.

* * *

When I was in my teens, I spent a lot of time with my Auntie Nina, the oldest daughter of David and Martha, after her husband "Baldy" Petersen died from a heart attack.

Nina told me of the hot summer day when she accidentally discovered her father having one of his liaisons. She had been shocked to her core. So well had my grandparents hidden the discord in their marriage that even Nina thought all was well until that day.

There was a woman in town whom people whispered about. She was a shaman, or so they said. Nina crept down to the woman's house and knocked on her door. Fort Yukon had no electricity then, and the bright summer sun made the unlit cabin seem dark by comparison. Back then people put heavy blankets over their windows to keep the hot, dry sun from turning their cabins into ovens.

From within the dark, cool cabin, the woman bade Nina to enter. When Nina told the woman about her parents and asked her to use her shamanism to change their behavior, the woman became angry. She screamed at Nina, who turned tail and ran. Never again would she attempt anything like that. Nina had to learn to accept the situation, for her parents had asked for neither her permission nor her approval.

I was neither shocked nor surprised to hear about by my grandfather David's affairs. He died years before my time, so I had never projected onto him any saintly images. But hearing Nina's story gave me a first glimpse into the fallibility of man and church.

CHAPTER THREE
Nina

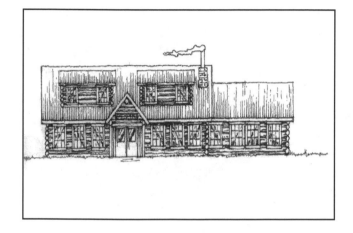

*D*avid and Martha "Itchoo" Wallis brought six children into the world. According to my Aunt Nina, the family lived a charmed life—when the epidemics allowed it.

By the 1910s, the Gwich'in people had shed their mooseskin attire and bedecked themselves in trousers, white shirts, and shiny black shoes. But as well dressed as they were, the Gwich'in were treated as primitives.

Piece by piece, the Gwich'in way of life was being destroyed. Religion—the thing closest to the human soul—was trod upon and redesigned; the culture was set aside; routines of daily life were obliterated. The preachers called shamanism a tool of the Devil. The missionaries frowned upon every habit the Gwich'in had that made him who he was. They spent many hours preaching, spanking, teaching, spanking, until the villagers learned that being Gwich'in was not a good thing.

The coming of the western culture did much to eliminate the Native lifestyle but the greatest threat by far was the epidemics: measles, smallpox, diphtheria, typhoid, tuberculosis, and influenza. These sicknesses wiped out thousands of Native Alaskans. In his essay *Yuuyarag: The Way of the Human Being*, Yupik leader and writer Harold Napoleon referred to these epidemics as the Great Deaths.

My Auntie Nina described one of the epidemics this way: "At first people wept for their loved ones, but after a while they were so numbed by their grief that when they carted another dead person to the graveyard, no one could weep."

This was the time she and my father were born into. Sickness and misfortune were constant dangers, and traditional Gwich'in beliefs conflicted with new Western ideas. Aunt Nina remembered when she was thirteen and had her first period. Her mother put her into seclusion.

It was an age-old belief that a girl in her first menses must be put into a special tent for a month. There, she would see only her mother, who would teach her the special rules of being a woman. A long, hooded bonnet was put on her head so that she could not see out of her peripheral vision in case she wandered outside. If the girl so much as glanced at a man during her first menses, she could jinx his hunting.

Auntie Nina told me that she sat in her lonely tent for one month. Her sisters Minnie and Ethel would drop by to visit and laugh at her in her bonnet. The two girls staunchly refused to take part in this tradition. Nina was only one of the sisters to believe what her mother taught her.

"You will live a long life," Itchoo told her.

Nina did peek directly at her father once as he returned from checking his traps. He winked at her. When she spoke of this moment, Aunt Nina's face flushed with pleasure. But she was also sure that the reason she had not succumbed to the epidemics, as her sisters did, was that she had respected this age-old belief.

When I was a child, Auntie Nina lived on the banks of the Yukon River with her husband, Vladimir, whom we called "Baldy" even though he had a full head of curly hair.

As a family, we were kept at a distance from them. Apparently there had been a sibling rivalry between Aunt Nina and my father. They could only stand one another occasionally.

Yet my siblings and I visited Aunt Nina all the time. She, like Itchoo, was a source of mystery. Her dresses always matched her socks, and a cardigan complemented her attire. But what really had us staring was a little doily she wore on her head that matched all her outfits. My mother said my aunt was self-conscious because her hair was thin on top. Whatever the reason, we saw her as an eccentric queen.

Auntie Nina was a collector of news clippings and bric-a-brac. She threw nothing away. When she put a new tablecloth on her heavy, round wooden table, she left the old one on underneath it. We counted the many colorful layers whenever we were allowed to sit quietly at the table.

Baldy did not encourage us to explore his house. His dogs intimidated us and rudely sniffed our private parts, so when we paid them a visit it was at our own risk.

I was seventeen when Baldy died, and after that I spent a lot of time with Auntie. Her only child, Larry, lived in Fairbanks, and she needed a companion. Although I was a poor partner, I was the only one in our family available to stay with her.

Baldy had been a jack of all trades. He loved making money. Everyone knew he bootlegged on the side. Once, when I was staying

Auntie Nina Wallis

with him and my aunt, some young men who came to the house got into an argument with him. I trembled in fear; the screaming and accusations got so loud I thought there would be violence.

After Baldy passed away, Nina tried to continue the business, for there were cases of booze left over. For a time I helped her bootleg the leftovers, but then she started drinking the stuff, and in no time we were broke.

Despite the fact that my aunt loved to tell stories, she was a lot like my father, unable to display her emotions easily. When her husband died, she became more melancholy. She often wept over the past, and I listened as she told me of people from long ago. This was how I heard of the epidemics.

One summer day, Auntie and I sought refuge from the hot sun in her big cool cache. As we dug through her stockpile of collected treasures, I came upon a small bundle. In the cloth were a dress, a lock of hair, and some other personal effects.

I asked Auntie, "What is this?"

Her usually placid features were overcome with remembered grief. In a moment, I knew I had breached a boundary into territory where I was not allowed. There was always this invisible wall that shut out us younger ones. We knew we had no emotional claims on our elders, yet part of us yearned to break through whatever it was that always kept us apart from them spiritually, even when we were physically close. I waited, not knowing how to react to this display of emotion. After Auntie collected herself, she told me her story.

She once had a daughter named Nina Clara, a child filled with laughter whom my aunt doted on. One day the girl came down with a fever. When Nina took her daughter to the hospital, the typhoid fever overcame the girl. Nina watched helplessly while her beloved child was pulled into death by raging fevers.

When hospital workers came to get Nina Clara's body to be put in the basement until burial, Auntie wept in denial. She did not want anyone treating her baby's precious body in an ungentle way. She followed them into the basement and kept vigil until the funeral. Burying her child was the hardest thing she ever had to do.

CHAPTER FOUR

Pete

My father, named Peter Trimble after an Episcopal bishop, never spoke of his past. It was from his sister Nina and from my mother that I learned about his life. He took all his emotions, sorrows, and loves to his grave in silence.

If it hadn't been for the stories that spread through word of mouth, I never would have known why my father had not wanted his children to speak Gwich'in. He and others like him had been made to feel ashamed of being Native. Teachers slapped their hands with a switch whenever they were caught using the Gwich'in language. Eventually Peter realized that to be Gwich'in meant pain and ridicule.

Long after my father died I discovered that he did not want us to be exposed to other people because he had witnessed the epidemics. He was afraid we would be exposed to disease; he didn't want to lose any more loved ones. But this he never told us, so we found his strict rules hard to understand.

As a youngster I heard no mention of the epidemics. But I noticed my father discouraged us from going to potlucks. When Uptown people celebrated an event, or cleaned the graveyards on Memorial Day, my brother Barry and I were the only ones from the family to attend, and we did so against my father's wishes.

In our family there were sick brothers and sisters from time to time. Once I contracted the mumps and had big swollen cheeks that ached and felt stiff. Even then I managed to chew greedily the chocolate bonbons that Itchoo bought for me, hurrying to eat them all before my siblings came home from school.

My father, born in 1916, had seen people die in masses. He had been in Fort Yukon during one epidemic when many white canvas tents were set up in front of the Hudson Stuck Memorial Hospital. The sick were so numerous that the impressive two-story log cabin, with many rooms and a solarium, could not hold them all. They died lying outside in the canvas tents.

"Pete," as everyone called him, helped by carrying wood and water. Pete was a robust child and avoided falling ill for a while. Then, without knowing how it happened, he awoke to find himself inside one of those canvas tents. The sun was hot, and he heard flies buzzing about.

That's my dad, Pete Wallis, on the left, with grandma "Itchoo" and Uncle Tim in this early picture.

He leaned unsteadily upon one elbow and looked around as if
waking from a strange dream. By his side was a bowl of something
that must have been soup but was then swarming with maggots.

The people tending the sick were too busy to check on many of
their patients. They were losing a war against this scourge, for when
the germs entered the body the sicknesses took a firm hold. With
their resistance low to the new bacteria brought by the white people,
most of the Natives had no chance.

Pete survived. It took him some time to regain his health. I imagine the hospital people being surprised by his recovery.

When epidemics came, many children were left alone as their
parents were sick. Often the parents died, leaving children behind as orphans. My grandparents survived the waves of sickness,
but lost three children. Martha watched her daughters Minnie and

Ethel and her son Grafton die. Then she had only Nina, Peter, and Timothy left.

For people like my grandmother who had seen so much, the loss of a loved one was felt deeply. Yet in their overwhelming love for those who lived, they often coddled and spoiled the remaining children with abandon, for tomorrow those children might die. This mentality clings to our culture even today.

People learned to live with a certain caution, though. This was the time when the Gwich'in people of our area fine-tuned their prejudices. The term "dirty Indians" was learned and used by our people. As I grew up I heard that term used by my father. Of course, as a child I was quite confused. I thought *we* were Indians. When I saw a drunk Native, I thought maybe this was the kind of person to which my father was referring. When I sought to question this, my mother hushed me. There was no questioning my father to his face, for that face easily became clouded with dark memories and resolve.

✳ ✳ ✳

When my father was sixteen, he was offered the chance to travel to England to live with his grandfather George Wallis and attend school.
But by that time he was solidly entrenched in village life and England seemed too far away. Instead, Pete remained in Fort Yukon to learn how to trap.

According to Aunt Nina, my father was taught wilderness skill by my grandmother Martha. She trapped off the land we call "*Neegoogwandaa.*" It is a piece of land twelve to fifteen miles from Fort Yukon, depending on whether you take the winter trail or the summer trail. An old man gave Itchoo this land after he became too old to trap. On the land is a large lake curved like the crescent moon, and within the curve is a mound of a hill. A fox had had her den there for a time, and so the old man and Itchoo called the trapline Foxhole Lake in the Gwich'in language.

There, Martha and her two sons, Pete and Tim, trapped their way into the economic world. David spent his days working for the church while Martha taught her sons the ways of the woods. Nina stayed near her father and kept his house for him.

When Martha and her boys came to town with furs to sell, they would pay their debts at the store and with what money they had left buy what they needed.

A few aspects of life in the village are not likely to change. One is that people will always have huge store bills to pay off, and the other is that there will always be bootleggers. At that time people bought alcohol from bootleggers and hid out in the woods to drink. To this day you can still find bottles hidden under moss and willow thickets.

Pete would seek out the bootleggers and spend his hard-earned money drinking.

Fort Yukon was like other early settlements across America. White people were determined to have law and order, and law and order did not include drunken Indians. Although this was not written in any law book, it was one of those laws understood across the land. If a Native was found staggering in the streets, he was thrown in jail without ceremony.

We siblings never knew anything about how my father spent his youth until my brother Barry took a job with the court system. There he discovered a long record of times my father had been thrown in jail for vagrancy.

At the time, we thought this meant that our father had been a vagrant, but later my mother explained that any Native found drunk was called that. All the white people could see were Natives who liked to drink, usually getting very drunk and becoming unsightly. They did not hesitate to label such Natives as vagrants and to put them behind bars.

Charges of vagrancy aside, Peter was a handsome man. Rumor had it that he may not have been David's son. Back then, people liked to point fingers at those suspected of infidelity. When the missionaries said don't do this and don't do that, people who were prone to doing this and that often pointed a finger and found four pointing back. It was a moral quandary for men and women, most of whom had been matched up in arranged marriages at a young age.

In any case, people whispered that Pete had been fathered by a white man that Martha had met in Circle City. Pete grew up with the nasty whispers and teasing from his peers until he developed a "to hell with it" mentality.

Before he met my mother, my dad fell in love with
a nurse, Freda Ribiloff, left, shown with her sister,
Jean. Freda died in a flu epidemic, and my dad
grieved for her the rest of his life.

With a survivalist outlook, he learned to be cynical. My father
frequently spewed his favorite sayings—especially when he was
drunk and wanted to show off his wit. I remember him saying boast-
fully, "If you can't impress a white man with your intellect, then dazzle
him with your bull." Of the Indians, he would say, "Give them a hand
and they try to take the whole arm."

I couldn't tell if he was serious or just loved to hear himself pro-
nouncing these clichés like a poet loves to quote poetry. But underneath his veneer of nonchalance, I sensed my father held emotions
in like a layer of earth holds back molten lava. A bitterness lay behind his words.

Despite his cynical attitude toward all the races that inundated
Fort Yukon, Pete had many friends. He also had affairs with many
women, and he fathered a few children; those offspring had to
remain a secret, for many of Pete's lovers were married women.
Perhaps it was his looks or his devil-may-care attitude that made

women seek him out despite his lack of commitment, but seek him out they did.

In those days, women watched movies starring handsome actors such as Cary Grant and Clark Gable. Men who, like Pete, had the slightest touch of good looks were highly sought after by women seduced by romantic films.

Pete's roving ways came to a stop when he met a young nurse named Freda at the Hudson Stuck Memorial Hospital. He and his buddies hid out in the woods and peeked at the young nurses who stood outside the hospital during their breaks.

Freda Ribiloff and her sister Jean had a mixture of Aleut and Russian blood, coming from Southcentral Alaska. They had been educated at Eklutna and found jobs working at the busy Hudson Stuck Hospital.

It was not long before both sisters fell in love and married. Jean found her soulmate in John Fredson, a Gwich'in man from Chandalar country who later used his education and status to turn Venetie into a reservation and to start its first school. Jean would support her husband through all of his dreams.

In Fort Yukon, Freda was Pete's love. He captured her heart and she his. Their love seemed to restore to them some of the innocence both had lost in the horrors of the epidemics.

Together they had a beautiful, curly-headed daughter named Ethel Marie. But what started out as a fairy tale soon was interrupted by another epidemic that took Freda's life and later took Ethel Marie's too.

There's no way of knowing what my father must have felt. I would have to travel back in time to witness his grief, to see how he shut down his emotions, protecting himself from a world infested with diseases that stole the one he loved.

In the years that followed, he would get drunk and sometimes I glimpsed his deep sense of loss. When my siblings and I struggled to find some affirmation of his love for us, I would see in his eyes a door closing, shutting us out.

He had made up his mind not to love, just in case.

CHAPTER FIVE
Hannah

*Y*ears before Peter Wallis lost his love Freda in Fort Yukon, a family very different from the Wallises lived on the Black River.

Moses and Hannah Peter lived in Chalkyitsik, sixty miles or so north of Fort Yukon. The Gwich'in word is *Jalgisick*, meaning "fish-hook" for the good fishing in the Black River, but today people spell the name Chalkyitsik. As children we use to call it "Chicklesticks" the same way we called our town "Fort Yuk" and Fairbanks "Frimbanks." It was our way to nickname everyone and everything.

Moses Peter had wed Hannah William in an arranged marriage. Back then, the older people took great delight in matchmaking, even if it was only in their minds that the match was perfect. Before contact, arranged marriages were a standard part of Gwich'in culture; girls had to comply with the wishes of their elders whether or not they liked the man selected for them.

Hannah William was a sultry beauty who had lived with relatives in Fort Yukon. When she came home, she was less willing to bend to the wishes of her mother, Maggie. Perhaps she was put out that her mother had remarried after her father's death, and she used that as an excuse to pout about her approaching marriage.

Like other Gwich'ins, Hannah was brought up to believe in Western values, yet she clung to past traditions. In the end, she obeyed Gwich'in tradition and married Moses Peter, who was totally with his reluctant bride. So it would always be. What's more, Hannah had another love, and her yearning for this other man caused her to act spiteful toward Moses.

In the first years of their marriage, Hannah gave birth to three boys, but all three died from disease. Hannah's daughter Mary then became the oldest child. Mary was sickly and spent much time in the Fort Yukon hospital and orphan ward.

After Mary, my mother, Mae, was born in Chalkyitsik on July 4, 1927. The fifth child, Mae was destined to become one of those resilient souls who would always be the strength behind those who were loud, boisterous, and weak in nature.

After two more daughters, Dorothy and Sarah, came a son, Edison. By then, the arranged marriage had soured, and Hannah told Moses that Edison was not his son. Moses reacted to Hannah's spitefulness by rejecting Edison.

My maternal grandparents, Moses Peter and
Hannah William, were joined in an arranged
marriage and had fourteen children.

Hannah often flew into fits of rage, especially when Edison wet
his bed or irritated her in some other way. Sometimes her anger came
for no reason other than frustration at her situation. In a foul temper
she would throw the little boy out of the house. Then Mae would take
his hand and lead him down to the house of their Grandmother
Maggie, where they would seek refuge until Hannah calmed down.

At Grandmother Maggie's, Edison and Mae inherited two treasures that would carry them into the future. One was the knowledge of how to make biscuits in a skillet atop a woodstove. While
they watched the dough turn a golden brown, Grandmother
Maggie told them stories from long ago. Her stories and her biscuits sheltered the two children from the harsh reality that awaited
them at home.

Their grandmother was angered by her daughter's ill treatment of Edison, but she would only scold Hannah lightly. Moses

was indifferent to the treatment Edison received because he believed what his wife had said about Edison not being his son.

Years later, as my mother sat by the side of her brother, comforting him as he slowly deteriorated from cancer, she would hold his hand and still see the rejected boy he had been.

∗ ∗ ∗

Mae's heart, always filled with compassion for her brother, drove her to find ways to shield him from Hannah's anger. At times she would get her share of unexplained beatings too. She never quite knew what to make of her mother's unpredictable behavior. Indeed, there were times when Hannah was sweet and reasonable, but then her mood would swing far to the right once more.

Slowly Hannah Peter's family was being fashioned around her moods. When he wasn't busy working to support his family, Moses helped with chores. But mostly it was the children who cut and chopped the wood and hauled water from the river in five-gallon buckets. They learned to do minor cooking, too, preparing biscuits, mush, or soup, in case their mother wasn't up to cooking that day.

Sometimes Hannah would act like a good wife and mother, but mostly she expected to enjoy time off from her responsibilities at home. People in the villages loved to play pan, a form of rummy, and mizhur, a form of bridge. Hannah spent hours upon hours playing these games.

The rare times when Hannah put someone besides herself first were when Mary came home for a break from the Fort Yukon orphanage, where she was treated for her childhood maladies. Mae never knew what kind of illnesses her older sister had, for at that time such things were hush-hush. She knew only that her family celebrated each time Mary returned from Fort Yukon.

Those visits were both good and bad for the Peter family. For Mary's homecoming, the house was cleaned to spotlessness, and fresh blankets, sheets, and pillows were dug out of storage for this favorite child. Hannah cooked, and Moses was happy.

Because Mary had been long separated from her siblings, she eyed them with great suspicion, an attitude she had learned living in the orphanage. She treated her siblings like inferiors, and they stood by and watched as she enjoyed treatment from their parents that they never received. When Mary pinched one of them out of spite, and the child wept, Hannah and Moses always took Mary's side.

Good food and festive atmosphere aside, it was always a relief when Mary left to go back to Fort Yukon. Then the clean sheets, blankets, and pillows were stashed away until the next visit. The pretense was over, and the other children could relax into their normal routine of packing in wood, carrying water, and helping with the other chores.

✳ ✳ ✳

As much as Hannah detested her situation in life, she tried to get used to it. Although she never did hard work herself, she could issue orders like a sergeant, commanding her children as if they were little soldiers. They brought in snow to be melted atop the stove for the washing; they were given the task of cleaning the diapers. Since Edison was the only boy, Mae and her two younger sisters, Dorothy and Sarah, had to help with all the outdoor chores too.

All the while Moses spent his time hunting and trapping to support the family. Once he took his daughters with him to an outlying cabin to trap muskrats. Their job was to check traps closer to the cabin while he went farther away to set traps. One morning he left early, saying he would spend the night at another cabin a long way off. Mae and her sisters were terrified of being left alone, but they had been trained to obey.

That afternoon, when they checked the traps on the lake in front of the cabin, they saw in the distance a large pack of wolves coming toward them.

"Let's go!" Mae said, running for the cabin, but Dorothy had dropped her packsack and tried to go back for it. Her sisters screamed at her, pulling her to the cabin.

The next morning, when Moses returned, he found the packsack chewed to tatters. He took the girls back to Chalkyitsik that day, out of danger from the large pack roaming the area.

In summer Moses would sometimes take his family to Fort Yukon in his wooden boat. The boat had an inboard motor with eight to ten horsepower, and it took days to reach the other village. There, Moses would sell his furs, buy more supplies for the winter, and fish along

The imposing old Hudson Stuck Hospital and Mission House
shows the influence of the Episcopal Church in our village.

the Yukon for food for his dogs. When there was demand for it, he
would cut wood and sell it to the hospital or the schools.

Most Native families were busy from early morning until late at
night. The older children would watch the younger children while the
mothers sewed products such as mittens, boots, slippers, and Indian
dolls to sell to outsiders. One Indian doll, perfectly dressed in the
style of pre-contact days, would bring a price of three to four dollars,
and for that a family could buy a case of canned evaporated milk for
its babies. Although Hannah detested physical chores, she, like most
other Native women, took great pleasure and pride in doing
beadwork, a skill taught by early missionaries and refined by the
Gwich'in. By selling their crafts, the women increased their income.

By the end of summer, the villagers would pack their families,
dogs, and supplies into wooden boats and go back up Birch Creek,
the Chandalar, or the Black River. If they didn't have a motor—a luxury
back then—they either paddled or lined their boats with pole and
rope along the riverbanks.

Once back in their home village, they would be busy until Christmas. There were moose to harvest, ducks to shoot, dried grass to

collect for dog bedding, and berries to pick. After freeze-up, trapping season arrived. The river and lakes were the main expressways; in order for trappers to travel, all the ice had to be frozen solid. Otherwise, people could find themselves crashing through an overflow—a thin layer of ice—into near-freezing water. Such an accident could be life threatening, so it was always best to wait until freeze-up was complete.

My mother said that Christmas, Thanksgiving, and Easter were unknown holidays to most villagers. Even during the Great Depression, people in isolated areas lived comfortably, for their lives always had been meager and they depended on none of the store-bought goods that people elsewhere stood in long lines to buy. It was from the schools that their children learned about Santa Claus, the Easter Bunny, and Christopher Columbus.

My mother remembered one holiday when she received a brand-new doll from the church. Each day after school, Mae rushed home and took the doll from where she had hidden it from her siblings. Then one day she pulled out her doll only to find it filthy. Her sisters had discovered the hiding place and had thoroughly enjoyed playing with the doll. Although Mae was unhappy about it, she understood how her sisters had been tempted. Hers was the only toy in the house.

Life in Chalkyitsik was quiet. There was no electricity and only one store. There was only solitude in the small settlement along the Black River. The children loved to play and hunt for small game along the lakes that dotted the land. Boys explored with boys, and girls stuck together. Parents knew they had nothing to fear from their children roaming the land. Once Mae and her sisters and friends wandered halfway to Fort Yukon, but they realized that they would get into trouble for going so far, so they ran all the way back to Chalkyitsik. Years after my mother married my father, she trapped the land between Fort Yukon and Chalkyitsik and she laughed to recognize the land where she had explored.

Many times the older women took any children who were old enough to walk with them to pick berries or to check snares and traps. My mother remembered walking to check muskrat traps with a bunch of women. Dogs carried packs upon their backs, patiently following.

An old woman was far ahead of the group when Hannah Peter looked up and saw a movement in the grass where the old woman had passed.

It was a grizzly bear. Quiet warnings spread through the group, and they snuck away before the bear spotted them. Then Mae and her cousin Alice were sent running back to the village to alert the men. The men went after the bear but only wounded it. It was never seen again.

At times, Moses tried to move his family to Fort Yukon. When his children first attended school there, they did not speak English. Mae remembered being ten years old. The Fort Yukon children helped her learn English. When the teacher tried to get her to say "cat" or "dog" by pointing at pictures, Mae responded in Gwich'in. That's when one of the boys took pity on her and explained in Gwich'in that she must try to say the words in English.

The first sentence Mae learned was "I am thirsty." She was so pleased with herself that she said it often around adults, hoping to impress them, but in response was handed glasses of water.

Fort Yukon was a busy place, and many families from neighboring villages tried to raise families there, but the traplines always called them back. So it was with Moses; he headed back to Chalkyitsik, which would always be his home.

One day as Hannah and Mae sat picking blueberries by Martin Hill, Hannah heard distant music. Old Gwich'in beliefs held that before one left this world, sometimes strange things happened. Snowy white owls would come to tell a person that his time was near. Sometimes people saw visions, or heard music. Gwich'in elders knew these things to be true but would not speak of them, especially not to children.

Near Martin Hill, Mae heard the vague music, too, before it faded away. Then she saw her mother hang her head, seeming to lose all interest in berrypicking.

"What's wrong?" Mae asked her, but Hannah would not tell her. They packed up their things and went home with their buckets only half filled.

Later, Mae mentioned this to her grandmother Maggie. The old woman's eyes took on a knowing look, then she shielded her emotions. Immediately Mae became curious. She knew that, in the back of their minds, the older people held beliefs that had become taboo.

Not long afterward, Hannah gave birth to her last child, a boy named Moses. The baby boy did not survive the birth, and neither did Hannah.

Hannah's children were told nothing about the mysterious music. All Mae was told was, "Your mother died in childbirth."

CHAPTER SIX
Mae

*A*fter all the years of living with his incomprehensible wife, arguing with her, loving her, Moses Peter was bereft at Hannah's death. He buried his wife in numbed grief, then allowed the local teachers to make arrangements for the care of his children.

The older children begged him to keep the family together.

"We have always done all the work," they pleaded, but Moses did not listen. He felt he was doing the right thing.

The Peter children were packed aboard a small plane. Older children were flown to Eklutna to attend school. The younger ones went to orphanages in Sitka and Seward, where they later died.

My mother remembered crying as her younger siblings, not understanding what was happening, held their hands out to her as they were lifted onto the plane. She never forgave her father for his indifference to their grief.

What made matters worse were his attempts to marry off Mae, at sixteen, to one of the local bachelors. To her most of the young men were like brothers. To marry one was unthinkable.

But Moses was determined to make arrangements for his children so that he would not have to worry about them. In Mae, he met with stubbornness. She thought it was unfair that her father would not allow her independence. Edison was barely fifteen but he was allowed to stay in the village. When Moses told Mae that he had lined up a husband, they got into a big fight, and he threw her out of the house.

Mae went to live with relatives. Many days passed before she realized her father was not going to change his mind. Either she would do as he wished or she would not be allowed to go home. Her cousins, feeling sorry for her plight, volunteered to take her to Fort Yukon.

Mae was young and knew that there was nothing left in Chalkyitsik for her. She packed her things, and that night the young boys took her by dog sled down the winter trail.

She would make Fort Yukon her home for forty-seven years, but when her cousins brought her to town that winter night, she was grief-stricken. In a short time she had lost her whole family, and Mae blamed her father for not saving the remnants of it.

Years later, grandpa would visit my mother and they would drink home-brew together. Mae would cry, asking him over and over why he didn't keep them together, why he kicked her out of the house. My grandfather would not know how to answer except to beg her forgiveness. They could display deep emotions only when they were drunk. When they sobered, it was as if they had never said such things to one another, until the next time they drank. Then they would go over the subject again.

∗ ∗ ∗

After her cousins left her with relatives in Fort Yukon, Mae vowed to save enough money to bring all her siblings back together. She was hired to work at the Hudson Stuck Memorial Hospital. The hospital employed many locals. Women served as assistants to Doctor Lulu Disosway in surgery, as nurse's aides in training, as cooks, or as dishwashers. Men provided the hospital with wood, water, and meat. While she was employed there, Mae cleaned, scrubbed, and even helped the doctor in surgery.

Dr. Lulu Disosway was a small, fiery woman. It was said that she once had quarantined Fort Yukon just before all the white trappers returned to town. At that time, the hospital had the authority to quarantine the village to control the spread of contagious disease. It was well known that when the trappers had cashed in their furs and paid their debts, suddenly they would become generous and share their booze with the Native population. Dr. Disosway frowned upon this generosity, seeing the Native people suffer from the resulting hangovers, black eyes, diseases, and unwanted pregnancies. Although the trappers suspected Dr. Disosway's quarantine, they dared not object. No one messed around when it came to epidemics.

Dr. Disosway had a dream of helping the Natives realize their potential. She wanted the girls who worked for her to go beyond what they thought themselves capable of, so she always offered them a chance to go to the States for further schooling in medicine. No one ever took her up on that offer, much to her disappointment.

My mother recalled that working at the hospital was a good job, but when Dr. Disosway performed any kind of surgery, mother wanted to gag from the stench of the blood. She and other girls like her could butcher and portion out a whole moose expertly, yet the sight of the

My mother and the other young
women in Fort Yukon bought shoes
and dresses at the NC Store to look
good for the weekend dances.

doctor operating on humans was too much to bear. It was gossiped that the doctor loved to operate.

The hospital and mission grounds were kept like estates. Green grass had been planted there along with an assortment of flowers. Long before Mae arrived in Fort Yukon the hospital had been built on ground near the river, but as the banks eroded away, the building was moved farther back. An engineer hired out of Seattle by the name of Neil Nicholson oversaw the monumental task of putting the huge building onto log rollers and using jacks and pulleys to propel it 500 feet north of its original position.

In Mae's time, employees of the Hudson Stuck Hospital were expected to work hard for wages of fifteen dollars a month plus room and board. Mae tried to save money, as she had promised herself she would, but even though fifteen dollars was a lot of money at that time, her money quickly dwindled. It dwindled even more quickly as she bought into the idea that she had to dress as well as her peers.

Back then, the dresses felt like they had crepe paper content, for they crackled, Aunt Nina and my mother recalled. My mother said that the shoes definitely had paper in them. When they got wet they fell apart. This was during World War II, when materials were in short supply and some clothing was made with cheap substitutes. Whatever the reason, such products ended up in the Fort Yukon store. The women of the village were determined to look good, so they bought the shoes and dresses to look their best for the weekend dances.

At first, Mae kept away from the nightlife. But the more operations she assisted with and the more pressure the good doctor put on her to be the one girl who would go away for medical training, the more Mae found pleasure in joining the other girls in going to the movie theater, which they called the showhouse.

It was fashionable to smoke then, as it is now. At the movie house villagers watched glamorous women and men holding cigarettes in their manicured hands. It was every girl's romantic dream to have a Cary Grant look-alike approach her with a lighter. Mae began to smoke Lucky Strikes. For the first time she was experiencing the freedom of being on her own and making her own choices.

When they were children, Mae and her sisters had looked through catalogs, wishing for the things inside. Mary was looking forward to having children so that she could dress them up in the many cute outfits. Mae listened as Mary talked of all the boys and girls she would one day have and how they would be raised. Mae swore then that she would never have children. She had witnessed the unhappiness in her home, and she knew that having a lot of children was work. But life has a way of changing your plans. Mary would never have children due to her ill health, and for my mother the future held fourteen of us, plus one miscarriage.

It was on one of her breaks at the hospital that Mae first saw Peter Trimble Wallis, the man who would cause her to break her vow.

* * *

By this time, Pete had been in the Army for a while and had been discharged due to a minor medical problem. While he had been away, his second wife left him. It had been a hasty courtship and impulsive marriage, so neither of them had been committed to one another.

Pete was handsome, like many of the men, but his air of nonchalance always struck women as vulnerability and innocence. He

had a lopsided smile. Even when he was thinking of nothing in particular, women perceived him as being a mysterious character.

From the moment she saw him, Mae was captivated. And the fact
that Pete was engaged to another woman did not deter Mae at all.

The fiancée was not from Fort Yukon, and she had an air of sophistication. Martha and Nina were looking forward to the impending marriage. They wanted Pete to settle down with a wife who would help
him raise his daughter Ethel Marie, whom my grandmother had been
caring for since Freda's death.

Mae volunteered to baby-sit. She befriended Ethel Marie, a lonely
little girl with only cousin Nina Clara to play with. Often when Mae
baby-sat Ethel Marie, Pete would come home, and finding her there,
he would talk with her.

At first, Pete saw Mae not as a prospective girlfriend but as a refuge from the responsibility that others called him to. He thought of
her as a pal. Even years later, when they were married and she went
to Tanana to have one of his many children, he would write her letters, signing off "Your pal, Pete."

Mae's crush on Pete deepened, and in time Pete began to look at
her in a new way. Her young age had been a deterrent, but as Mae
pursued him, he adjusted to the idea. He told her he was five years
older. Actually he was eleven years older.

When he first tried to kiss her, Mae backed away.

"What's the matter?" Pete asked her.

After a while, she confessed that her mother had told her never to
let a man kiss her or she would become pregnant.

Pete was amused by this and laughed heartily. He assured her
that this was not true, and he bent his head to kiss her.

$$* * *$$

Not long after that first kiss Mae realized she was pregnant.

When she told Pete, he did not react, at least not on the surface.
He was good at hiding his feelings. This angered Mae, yet she believed he loved her.

When Pete's fiancée discovered he was having liaisons with Mae,
the woman left town. Martha and Nina, their plans for him dashed,
burned with resentment toward Mae. No woman in her right mind

would take back a man who had impregnated another woman. Meanwhile, Pete acted the knave and refused to marry Mae.

After their daughter Hannah was born, Mae realized she was not in a socially acceptable situation. People were beginning to ostracize her. Whispers circulated when she passed by, and still Pete refused to marry her. He stated flat-out that he would never marry again.

As gentle as her usual nature was, there came a time when Mae became a roaring storm. When she broached the subject and Pete answered with a sulking silence, she challenged him.

They even got into fights. Mae was no match for Pete physically, but she outmatched him in her determination and stamina.

One day, they had a big fight, and he hit her in the face, giving her a black eye. Mae had to wonder if hers was a lost cause, and she was just entertaining thoughts of leaving Pete when he came in and announced that he had set up a wedding.

"Put this dress on." He tossed at her a yellow dress that his sister Nina had provided.

"What about this?" Mae asked, pointing to her black eye.

He dug around on a shelf for a pair of sunglasses. And so my mother went to her wedding wearing a yellow dress and sunglasses.

Years later, when she told this story to us little listening children, she laughed at how ridiculous it sounded. I was saddened that my father had spoiled the story by hitting her. Even then, I knew it healed my mother to talk to us about her painful past. We loved her very much, and when my father came home I would glare balefully at him with clenched fists. My mother always told the truth, no matter how much it hurt, and that affected how I told stories when I grew up.

CHAPTER SEVEN
Siblings & Seasonal Friends

*A*fter Pete and Mae's wedding, more children came. My mother said that after three daughters—Hannah, Clara, and Linda—my father threatened divorce. He wanted boys.

He said it teasingly, but he was a little serious, too. Traditionally, males had been favored as potential hunters who provided for the tribe. This mentality still clings to our culture, although to a lesser degree.

Eventually David was born, then Johnny, Grafton, and Jimmy. Grafton was the boy who died later in an accident. I don't remember him, but others have told me that after his death Martha and I used to stand outside and cry out for him.

Martha was the sister born next. Then I was born, followed by the five siblings who we would come to refer to as the five B's: Barry, Billy, Brady, Benny, and Becky.

Before they settled permanently in Fort Yukon in 1959, my father and mother were nomadic. They moved back and forth between Fort Yukon and Neegoogwandah for a number of years. Trapping was the only way a man could support his family then, and hunting helped him to feed his children. Many times my grandmother followed them up to Neegoogwandah, where she set up camp nearby and trapped for herself.

My mother said that she and my father bought their staple goods at the Northern Commercial on credit and paid the bill after trapping season. Sometimes they chartered small bush planes out to their trapline; that would run up a large bill that had to be paid with trapping money.

My mother's best memories of life with Pete are of living out in the woods together. My father was at his best when he was living off the land. In Fort Yukon he was drawn uptown to his buddies, with whom he would drink for weeks at a time.

In time the older children had to attend school, and my parents decided to live in Fort Yukon full time. My mother purchased a house from a couple that had moved to Fairbanks, and there my parents made a home.

✳ ✳ ✳

As is the case in most large families, certain children within the fold develop bonds, while others scarcely acknowledge each other. My younger brother Barry became my playmate. In rough times we stuck together. As my childhood buddy, Barry had to play dolls with me, and he did so without complaint.

My older sister Martha enjoyed playing with Jimmy. Jimmy had been very close to our brother Grafton, but after Grafton died, Jimmy and Martha filled the void by playing together.

Playing with Jimmy made Martha into a tomboy. She would have nothing to do with me or with the dolls she abandoned. Instead she ran around with a toy gun in her cowboy holster. Martha and Jimmy—who I compared to the mischievous Siamese cats in the Walt Disney movie *Lady and the Tramp*—often grew tired of playing cowboy and Indian, and in their boredom would look for ways to torment Barry and me. They never really picked on Barry because he managed not to overreact, but I was easy to scare, easy to tease, and therefore a good victim. Barry would stand on my side and quietly let them know which side he was on.

Another favorite playmate was a neighbor boy named Timmy, who was being raised by his grandpa. Timmy loved playing with dolls and doing other girl stuff. We didn't tease him, for he was strong in his preference—and he was older than we were. Besides, I enjoyed his interest in dolls and in housekeeping.

Timmy had been left behind by his mother, and his grandmother had died, so he was cared for by his grandfather, an old man who drank too much. For some reason I was never able to discover, my father detested this arrangement, and he didn't want us to play with Timmy at all. So whenever our father was not around, we played with Timmy. Children do not come to hold their parents' prejudices until much later.

One time, I got mad at Timmy when I thought he had stolen my doll. Three of my siblings and I shared a godmother named Mary Ee-ah. Back then people were often named according to a physical trait, and our godmother had a slight cleft lip that gave her voice a nasal sound. Mary Ee-ah was fond of us. Having four godchildren was quite a responsibility, and she attended to it with much seriousness. Each Christmas, even when she could not afford it, she would give us one present to share. Once the gift was a black doll with shiny curls. The three siblings with whom I shared Mary Ee-ah did not like the doll, so it was with much joy that I took this doll into my growing collection.

One day the doll disappeared. I decided the only other person who liked that doll was Timmy, so he became my suspect. When I confronted him, he clenched his fist and in an insulted tone denied my accusations. I backed off immediately, for he was bigger. When I took the problem to my parents, they shrugged it off as insignificant. As much as I hated to, I had to give up the search for my missing doll, but I would not relinquish her memory.

Perhaps because I was in a large family where children were sometimes ignored out of sheer necessity, I became very sympathetic toward my dolls—and the dolls my sister Martha discarded. The dolls were my children. This protectiveness sometimes bordered on an obsession.

At night while we slept in the back room of our two-room cabin, one of my mother's duties was to keep the woodstove burning. When the cabin cooled, I used my blanket to cover all twelve dolls. They had no clothes, and I feared they were cold. My maternal instincts would have it no other way. Awaking in the night, my mother found me curled into a little ball, and in exasperation she would take the blanket off the dolls and cover me with it. By some instinct, I would wake up to cover up my dolls again.

This struggle continued all through the night. In the morning, as my mother cooked our mush and pancakes, she would scowl at me. Although as a young child I was not one to talk back to my mother, I became brave when it came to my dolls. To my mind they were cold and needed my protection.

Martha and Jimmy must have sat by many a breakfast, listening in great amusement to my mother and me having this ongoing discussion. They must have decided to put an end to all this. I didn't suspect a thing until one summer day I ran to the outhouse behind the cabin.

Going to the toilet, indoors and outdoors, was a nightmarish experience. In the house behind the woodstove we kept a chamber pot that looked like a big white soup pot with a red rim and cover. It was usually full, stinky, and hot from the woodstove. Blessed was the day it was clean—then I did not want to contaminate it. When the stove was too hot, I feared tipping the potty accidentally and falling on to the stove with the stinky stuff all over me. Although it was a dangerous place to put a potty, others in the family preferred to keep the pot behind the stove for privacy. There were no walls save for a curtain that one of my older sisters occasionally put up as a statement of individuality.

But the outhouse held the most fears. Many times I wished that I didn't have to go potty at all. The rough-cut pieces of lumber of the outhouse floor were spaced sometimes an inch apart, and through the cracks you could look down and see the bottomless pit. At least, that's what it looked like to us children. The toilet seat was too high, and no one had thought to put a stool nearby for children. We had to climb very carefully, hoping not to catapult ourselves accidentally through the large oval hole someone had fashioned with saw and sandpaper.

I always forgot to rip a few pages out of the Sears Roebuck, Montgomery Ward, or Aldan catalog before climbing up on to the toilet seat. Some considerable leaning and reaching took place on the precarious perch before I could tear off half a page. It was always a pain to use the hard, brittle, glossy pages. I suspected that older people were hoarding the much softer black-and-white pages, which were always missing. In the ice-cold winter months, the glossy pages froze, and the resulting scratches and paper cuts could be deadly to your behind. No amount of rubbing and crumbling softened these pages.

On that summer day, as I entered the small house of doom, I went through the ritual of cautiously opening the door lest a hornet lunge out at me or lest there be another sibling on the seat—or, worst yet, my father, whose quick temper I feared. But the toilet was empty. As I entered, I vaguely noticed that a string was hanging halfway down from the ceiling. I pulled my pants down and leaned over to climb atop the seat. It was then that I saw my dolls, lying in a heap at the bottom of the toilet hole.

I let out a blood-curdling scream that must have reverberated throughout the neighborhood.

My mother ran out of the house, wiping her hands on her dirty apron and bounding toward me.

"What is it?" she asked. I could not speak as tears ran down my face. I pointed to the toilet hole.

My mother looked down the hole. "That damned Martha and Jimmy!" she exclaimed angrily. It was then I noticed the string hanging down. Looking down at my dolls, their heads severed from their bodies, I realized that they had been lynched.

I bawled louder, and my mother assured me that she would punish the culprits as soon as she caught them.

The look on her face and the cussing that ensued made me believe that she would bring about justice. Now I suspect she said it more to gain some peace and to comfort a child crying over a bunch of dolls. In the corner of my eye, I thought I glimpsed the two murderers slinking gleefully off into the woods nearby; they would lay low until they knew it was safe. In my heart I knew my mother could not punish anybody severely.

Children are very strong, and in time of trauma they can move on if love enables them to heal. Although we were a large family and I only spent time around half of my siblings and my mother, plenty of love came my way at the time I lost my dolls, and I soon forgot all about them.

But Martha and Jimmy were not through with their mischief, and it seems I was always to be their unwitting victim. When Jimmy was elsewhere, Martha found her own ways of getting a good laugh.

One day, Mom asked Martha and me to take a note down to our Aunt Nina, who lived at least a block and a half away. We jumped at this opportunity. Since losing our brother Grafton our parents rarely let us out of their sight. Martha said she needed to use the outhouse first. Mom went back into the house and I waited outside.

I waited and waited. Waiting in a treeless yard, sitting on the dirt, on a clear summer day in Fort Yukon, you feel how hot the sun can be, especially when there's no breeze.

When I tired of waiting, I hollered for Martha to hurry up. There was no answer, so I waited longer. My patience soon ran out and I approached the outhouse, impatiently demanding that my sister finish.

There was no response, so I pestered some more. Still no answer. Finally I peeked through the rough-cut lumber and was astonished to find the outhouse empty.

I was not the only child who feared falling down the toilet hole. We all shared that fear. So when I looked in the toilet to find that my sister was gone, I tugged on the door, only to find it locked from inside. I panicked so loudly that my mother came flying out of the house again, wiping her hands on her apron. In between gasps and sobs, I told her what was wrong.

Terror came over my mother's face, and she tore at the locked door.

"Martha! Martha!" she screamed, pulling at the door as I stood by crying.

Mom looked wildly around the yard for a stick. Finding one by the woodpile, she slid it into the crack and lifted the hook up, yanking the door open. We both ran inside and looked down the hole, finding nothing but crap at the bottom. Definitely no Martha.

It was then that we heard a wheezing sound behind us. We turned to see Martha holding her stomach as she looked at us through a haze of laughter.

It took Mom a full moment to regain her senses and become angry. She grounded both of us. I went into the house crying because it was Martha who should have been punished. Although Martha regretted not being allowed to leave the yard, she gleefully relished her prank as I pouted the rest of the day away.

✳ ✳ ✳

We lived a quarter of a mile from the Yukon River, the fifth-largest river in the world. In the 1960s, before a dam was put up to divert the river's frequent flooding of our village, and long before the erosion dams were set along the banks in the early 1990s to prevent Fort Yukon from falling into the river, the water was untamed and ruthless. Each spring, huge cakes of ice crashed and splintered along the riverbanks. People stood in awe, watching nature at its most powerful.

We younger Wallises were never to leave the yard unless we were accompanied by an adult or had special permission. To reinforce this rule, my father gave us memorable whippings if he caught us leaving the yard. It was always Barry and me who risked leaving and Martha who tattled on us whenever she discovered our absence.

The worst spankings came when we were found near the river. You would think that if your father spanked you senseless you would learn to listen, but sometimes the forbidden no matter how danger-ous is more powerful than your sense of self-preservation. Barry and I were always getting caught playing near the river, or sometimes just sitting daydreamingly on an overhang, staring entranced into the swirling eddies below.

We had a secret path out of our yard. In front of our cabin stood tall, dry grass the color of wheat. We would go into the tall grass and pretend for a while to be playing in it. When we were sure no one was looking, we would make a mad dash toward a bunch of willows and spruce trees. Then all we had to do was get across the road without being spotted. After that we would go along a ditch where the Stuck hospital had once stood, and follow the ditch to the river bank. Once our father's boss spotted us and chased us home, but thankfully he never told.

✳ ✳ ✳

There was no season that we village children did not enjoy. Win-ter was for digging tunnels and mazes in the snow berms that the village tractor made as it cleared the roads. It was so much fun that we played until we were nearly frozen. When we pestered our par-ents for dry socks and mitts, they threatened us that next time we would have to stay inside. By the stove and hanging on the indoor clothesline were dripping socks and mittens that sorely tested my mother's usual patient demeanor.

Not wanting to stay indoors, which was seen as a personal dis-grace, we took turns warming up here and there in different neighbor's homes.

At night we played in darkness. There were no orange beams of light to guide us, as there are today. Most homes had a few bulbs that hung from rudimentary light fixtures. The stars that illuminated the snow kept us company. When the Northern Lights swirled above, we were filled with fear, for we believed that the lights could come down and take us. But when the moon was out we were like rabbits, hop-ping and skipping until almost ten at night, when we were forced to come inside to sleep.

In winter, we made tunnels through the snow berms
alongside the village roads.

All winter our house was steamy from the fish and moose meat
that always seemed to be cooking on the stove. The other dominant
smell was of frozen laundry. After washing, my mother would hang
the laundry out. When certain items were needed, she would bring
them in to be thawed and dried on the indoor clothesline. The fresh
scent filled the cabin. Once a week our blankets were hung out for
the day and at night we buried our noses in them, relishing the fresh,
cool scent of the outdoors.

The two-room log cabin seemed large to us, but in reality it must
have been tiny, for our older siblings slept in another cabin nearby or
stayed with relatives. We made hideouts and tunnels under the big
hospital bed where my father slept in the front room, and under
our wooden beds in the back. My mother kept storage boxes under the beds, and we dug through them in curiosity. Sometimes
we made beds in the boxes of clothes, and the boxes served as
pretend houses. My parents did not care, for there so many of us,
and any time we were occupied playing under the beds for hours
at a time, they were grateful.

On one side of the front room, a homemade hutch and table with a utensil drawer, and a woodstove, served as our kitchen. On the other side of the room was my father's bed and some chairs for visitors.

In the hutch was plenty of space for us children to hide, and while playing house we would taste-test all the bulk food stored there. We loved munching on elbow macaroni and sweet rice, but we were really lucky if we found prunes or raisins. Then, like the mice that occasionally robbed my mother's larder, we would sit there and eat until all the treats were gone.

My mother spun a story about the little knothole on the side of the cupboard that looked like an arched doorway. She said that doorway belonged to the mice. Trying to scare us to sleep at bedtime, my mother would warn us that the mice would get us, and we would quiet down, listening for them. My older sisters said my mother used that old trick on them too when they were little, and that when they saw a mouse for the first time, they were surprised how small it was.

We were charmed by the stories. During the long, cold winter nights, when my mother settled us down to sleep, she told us about the past. At the time we did not connect the stories to our own ancestors, for she referred to them as Indians. At the showhouse we often watched movies about cowboys and Indians. We thought of Indians as those people in loincloths and braids who killed cowboys using hatchets and bows and arrows. We were frightened of the savages who killed those poor cowboy people. In fact, we hated those ruthless Indians. It would be years before we would come to see the other side of the story.

Sometimes when she was bone weary from a long day, my mother would try to shorten her stories, but we would get her back on track, for she had told all her stories to us many times. Despite her weariness, she would laugh at our knack for remembering every detail of her sometimes long stories.

When my mother was too tired to tell us a story, she would quiet us down another way. She would tell us that our tribal enemies were nearby— the Eskimos, who used to raid our land. Then we would hide under our blankets in fear. Years later I attended a Job Corps school out of Astoria, Oregon, and met an Eskimo girl there. She said that at bedtime her mother used to tell her not to make noise or the Indians would hear and come for her.

✳ ✳ ✳

My parents tried to make our lives interesting despite the difficulty of raising thirteen children with little money. We kept a cardboard box filled with socks that did not have mates, and my mother got us to match them up. This did wonders for our color coordination. My father put up rose-colored wallpaper from the store and we spent the winter drawing on the walls. In springtime he replaced the paper as we sharpened our pencils.

My mother made our clothes, and what she could not make was donated to her. She made our canvas boots for the winter. The boots had thick mooseskin on the bottom for durability, and the canvas uppers were decorated smartly with fancy rickrack. The uppers had braided yarn inside a seam to keep out the snow, and there were skin laces to tie snugly around the ankles. Insoles kept our toes cozy and warm.

Every now and again, there were store-bought jackets that were never too warm. Mostly we wore parkas our mother made out of corduroy fabric with fiberfill and a fur ruff on the hood to keep the cold off our faces. We used our knitted scarves as jump ropes or to hitch puppies to a sled. One year, we stuffed our hats with clothing to make a ball and tied it to the clothesline pole with our scarves to play tetherball.

Our toys were almost all improvised. Once a friend came to play, bringing a whole set of toy dishes. My little cardboard box was filled with mayonnaise jar covers for plates and empty soup cans for cups. My friend stared quietly at my dishes while I waited greedily to play with hers.

I remember a friend of my mother's and sisters' sending a whole wardrobe of expertly made Barbie Doll clothes for my tattered Barbie. There was even a fashionable coat with a mock fur collar. My Barbie was Cinderella that winter.

We never thought of ourselves as lacking things, for my mother challenged us to take what we had and see what we could make of it. In winter, she would send us out in search of clean snow. To this she would add vanilla, cream, and sugar, and we would have ice cream.

I'm the toddler in this photo with four older siblings including Grafton, left, who was killed in an accident.

Sometimes she poured straight sugar into melted grease to make sugar daddies.

We learned to make use of all the boxes and wrappings from store-bought food. We always vied for the Sun Maid girl on the boxes of raisins and for Betty Crocker's face so we could pretend she was our mother. We felt blessed to get our hands on a Cracker Jack box so we could cut out the little sailor. Sometimes, if my mother had time, she would make paper cutouts of people or a dog team. My father sometimes carved wooden boats, complete with motors, out of driftwood for the boys. When Christmas came and we received presents, our plastic toys lasted a few days and we ended up playing with our old toys again.

The list of games we played was long and varied with the seasons, and there was not a day we were bored. In summer, our parents allowed us to stay up playing late into the bright northern night. With a long, dark winter ahead, they wanted us to absorb as much sunlight as we could, and after playing all evening we would sleep well into the day. At noon, as we began to stir, my mother would place thick wool blankets over every window to keep out the sunshine and she would open the front and back doors to create a draft through the cabin. We could hear the maintenance man mowing the yard of the clinic, and the smell of fresh-cut grass would mix with the scented summer breeze. Then we would start our whole day over again knowing it would last long into the night.

Many games came from outside our culture and somehow got renamed when we played them. For instance, there was Ante, Ante, Over, which we called Andy, Andy, Over. That's the game where two groups stand on opposite sides of a house, and then a ball is thrown over the roof. If it is caught, then the person who catches it rushes to the other side to see how many people he can tag with the ball. Those tagged have to join the other side. This game is played until everyone is on the same side.

Another game was Red Rover, Red Rover, which we called Red Over, Red Over. All the neighborhood kids would choose sides, and the two teams would face each other, holding hands in a line. One team would call a person from the other team over. That person would try to break through the line of hands. If he couldn't break through, then he had to join that side. If he did break through, then he could take a person to his side.

For another game we drew a huge circle in the dirt. All the kids would gather on one side, and one person with a ball would try to tag someone. Whoever got tagged had to come out of the circle, and the last one in the circle was the victor.

Our favorite game was Kick the Can. We would put one can on a piece of board, and one person would be "It." One of the children would kick the can as hard as he could and the person who was "It" would rush to get it and place it back on the board. Everyone else would hide. He would look around and if he spotted any kids after the can touched the board, those kids were out. They had to wait for someone to kick the can and let them hide again. This was done until the person who was "It" could get everyone out.

Once when we were playing Kick the Can, I cheated and hid in Mary Thompson's house. While Mary told stories to me as she deftly knitted socks and smoked cigarettes, I looked out the window, watching the others search for me in vain. Needless to say, after that they did not trust me to play fair.

Traditional games were played, too, but they always took some special effort. When my father had spare time, he would take the hip bone of a beaver, which has a hole where the joints connect, and tie it to a sharpened willow stick with a string. We would spend hours tossing the bone into the air and trying to catch it on the stick through the hole.

∗ ∗ ∗

In the summer, we spent every waking moment with our friends. I remember one time when I couldn't poop, my mother gave me an enema. All of the neighborhood kids gathered around the big wooden bed to watch, like medical students learning a new procedure.

When my mother had no medical solution for our ailments, it came in handy to have the clinic just behind our house. One time as my mother rushed my brother Billy to the clinic because he had gotten a big sliver in his knee from our floor, he howled in pain and begged my mother to let him die at home.

At other times we had to nurse ourselves—especially when we accidentally ran into a bee's nest and got stung all over. Then we would run to the brown willows and take down the shiny, green leaves to chew. They tasted bitter but helped keep the swelling down.

We Downtown children did almost everything together. The only thing we weren't allowed to do was to have sleepovers. But in the day we took turns getting snacks from our families' houses. We ate Pilot Boy crackers, raisins, biscuits, and whatever else we could find in our parents' cupboards. Sometimes our fathers would leave their grub-box outside in the porch, and we would raid that. These wooden, trunk-like boxes carried all the kitchen and food items an outdoorsman would want on a hunting trip.

Sometimes our fathers bought fifty-pound bags of dog food and we even tried to eat that. When my mother caught us she was positively scandalized. She never wanted us to be *that* hungry. We always thought we were being daring and funny.

In late July and August, we stood in thorn bushes and ate rosehips, which we call *neetsi*. Sometimes we found high-bush cranberries nearby. We collected those to take home and put a spoonful of sugar on them. The sweet and sour combination was delicious.

Then the sun began to cast long shadows upon the land, and we watched mournfully as our friends and their parents prepared to leave Fort Yukon. We knew that summer had come to an end.

CHAPTER EIGHT

*a*t the end of summer, we Downtown children prepared to go to the local school, far up on the hill. Our school was built in 1958, about the same time as the Air Force station a mile above Crowtown. The school was a long structure that housed all the classes from kindergarten to high school.

I was introduced to the school when I was three or four. I remember an older sister taking me for the long walk uptown. The Air Force oiled the streets to keep the dust down, and as I held onto my sister's sweaty hand I could hardly breath for the fumes that rose into my nostrils.

When we entered the school building, I was met by a beautiful young woman, Miss Beasley, who would be my teacher. Instantly I became shy. I had never seen anyone like her before. She had brown hair in a bouffant hairdo. She wore a short skirt. I had never seen so much skin exposed. Gently she led me into the classroom and my shyness overcame me, for all the Uptown children stared at me in silence. I knew none of them.

Two women from the village had been hired to help. I recognized Delia Williams with her quick smile and lively eyes; she was a friend of my parents and often visited. She was the school cook. Every day at about two in the afternoon, we drank milk and snacked on peanut butter piled on a Pilot Boy cracker. Sometimes she served dried prunes or bananas. These were foods we did not get at home. At home we ate off the land: rabbits, muskrats, fish, moose, and beaver meat. Whenever we were allowed to sample outsiders' cuisine, we did so greedily.

The other woman was Nina Flitt, the bilingual teacher. She taught us phrases in Gwich'in, for despite our village accent, we were strictly English speakers. I remember one phrase she taught us: *vun gwinzee*, good morning. We had to say *vun gwinzee* each morning when our teachers entered the room.

Most of the children were from Uptown; a few lived in between Uptown and Downtown. As a child from the Wallis family, I rarely strayed far from home and knew only the children from Chalkyitsik who lived in downtown Fort Yukon during the summer. The Uptown children seemed different. I don't know what was different about them exactly, but somehow they were different. Perhaps I was the one who was different.

Once, when the teacher's aide tried to put me back into line, I balked and pulled away. She grabbed me roughly by the collar, and the next thing I knew we were fighting. Without knowing how I did it, I ripped her shirt, exposing her bra. The other children stared at me in silent shock.

On another day, when I awoke late from a nap and went around the long building to the playground, the other children laughed at my tardiness. I fled in tears and could not be consoled. My sister happened to be in the neighborhood and took me home. She wanted me to fit in and berated me for being a crybaby. I was still drinking from a bottle, and all I knew was that when I got home I would ask my mother for a warm bottle of milk and go to sleep.

After summer school ended that year, I never saw Miss Beasley again. But one summer around noon, I was shaken out of sleep and handed a flat brown package from her. Inside was a book in the shape of a bear, telling the story of The Three Bears. I opened the book, pressed it to my nose, and breathed in its newness. Perhaps the book later became torn and abused, but I'll always remember it as brand new.

$$* * *$$

So began my school years. I got used to the Uptown children, but I maintained my loyalties. Actually, after a while I became confused about whose side I was supposed to be on.

For instance, I was from Downtown, and that meant if we were having a mini-war, then I was to side with the Downtown kids. But there was also a sharp division among the white kids, the Indian kids, and the half-breeds. No one could figure out where the Wallis children fit in, so we had to be in the middle most of the time, but when push came to shove we had to choose sides. It was complicated.

Once a bully in our class decided it was time to teach some blond half-breeds a lesson, so he formed a gang. He told my childhood friend Patty and me that we were to join his side or else.

Patty and I were helping chase the kids downtown to their house when all of a sudden one of their older brothers and his pals came between us—and they were bigger. We stopped. While they were exchanging words, Patty and I tried to blend in with the same kids moments before we were trying to cream. They noticed and told their big brother, but he had a soft spot for children and let us off easy. It was all politics.

The kids from our town had watched too many James Dean and Marlon Brando movies, and they tried to emulate these tough characters. Unfortunately, those of us who did not have a gang mentality were forced to join or get a beating for our cowardice.

Some of the kids were downright hostile. There was no telling what happened in their home life, but they seemed to have an innate meanness. Those of us who were not fighters by nature had to be on the lookout, and we were as jumpy as rabbits.

One particular bully loved picking on those who were smaller. He must have been held back in school a few years, for he towered above all of us. He had a mean streak that would not quit, and he had a habit of licking his knuckles when he was about to pummel someone. Perhaps he threatened other children besides me, but there were times I felt that I was the only one. He lived in the center of town, and made a point of guarding the roads when we came home so he could try to beat us up. In all the years he wanted to beat me up, he was never able to catch me.

Once I heard some whispering in class when the teacher was not looking. I looked up to see some kids exchanging notes while staring my way. The Bully held up one hand and smacked it with a fist—and my worst fears were confirmed. My turn had come.

School got out each day at four. Fifteen minutes before the bell rang, my mind frantically formed a plan. Every moment would be crucial, for if I made one small mistake, I would feel those wet knuckles on my face.

The minute the bell sounded, I took off. I ran from classroom to classroom, collecting my three younger brothers whom I had to take home each day. In hurried tones I explained to them our dilemma.

We ran down the road to the airport where my father worked downtown, at the foot of the hill. The fumes from the oiled-down road rose into our noses and choked our breathing as we ran on shaking legs.

We had a head start on the bullies, but they were after us in full flight. My little brothers hung tightly to my sweating hands as we gasped raggedly for air with those big boys making all kinds of threatening noises behind us.

Fear was my ally that day, for it filled my bloodstream with adrenaline. As I pulled my brothers down the road, my mind frantically sought a way out of this. We were small, and my brothers were exhausted from the one-mile sprint. I knew those boys would have us any minute, so I stopped and turned to face them with the only weapon I had: my mouth.

They slowed to a walk and came within five feet of me. The Bully came closer, although he too was perplexed.

"If you guys lay a hand on me and my brothers, my father said he would kill you!" I said vehemently. (What my father actually had said was "You hafta learn to fight your own fight.")

The Bully came closer, but doubt flickered over his face.

"She's lying," he said "Her father doesn't care."

I knew he was looking for a hint of vulnerability in me, so I stood my ground, looking sure of myself. Inside I was quivering like a bowl of jelly. But as we faced off, the others lost their steam and turned to leave, as if I would not have been fair game anyway. The Bully threw me a look that said he would bide his time.

The next time I was chased by the Bully, I was alone. Although small, I ran fast and even managed to hit the Bully in the mouth with a rock—which not only raised my status as a fighter but also increased my chances of getting seriously injured in the future.

From first to the sixth grade I had to avoid the Bully's fists. There were others who would hit me, kick me, bury my head in the snow until I turned blue, and verbally abuse me until I cried, but they were lightweights compared with the Bully. I thought if he ever caught me I'd have to be hospitalized afterward. It took great care and diligence to make sure the Bully never got his hands on me.

My final encounter with the Bully came the winter before I turned twelve. After years of threatening to get me good, he had never done it.

Linda, my third-eldest sister, had married and given birth to a wonderful little boy whom we all loved to hold and cuddle. But to get to Linda's house we had to sneak by the Bully's house. One quiet Saturday afternoon, I ventured uptown to see my baby nephew.

Just when I thought I was in the clear, the Bully came out of no-where, licking his knuckles. In his eyes I could see that he planned to even the score for all those years I had cleverly avoided his fists.

By then the Bully was a teenager, and I had overheard my father and his friends commenting on how this particular youth would end up in jail sooner or later for breaking into people's houses. As the Bully was about to take me by my collar and smack me, I said quickly, "If you lay a hand on me, you will go to jail!"

His fist stopped in mid-air and a look of profound doubt came over his face. I knew this boy had passed beyond the boundaries of childhood and been exposed to more than I could imagine. My words were losing their power over him, so I spoke with as much authority as I could muster.

"Already you have broken into Della's house, and the police are looking for you. If you hurt me, there will be one more charge against you, and they will put you on a plane and send you away."

These words made him drop his hands. I cautiously walked away lest he decide to smack me after all, but he did not follow. I turned to look back. He was still standing there.

✳ ✳ ✳

Fights were not only personal. There were gang fights, too. Those of us who hated fighting were called to duty when the Uptown kids fought with the Downtown kids. I never knew who or what had started the fight; I only knew that if I refused to participate I might be seen as a traitor. Just when I thought I had the rules down pat, something changed my mind.

Once, all the kids were whispering excitedly about a rumble about to take place. I did not know what there was to be excited about, for fighting was ugly, but everyone was slinking around with crazed looks. After school, I took one of my little trails through the woods, fully in-tending to sneak all the way downtown without getting involved.

There on my path were three big boys kicking one of the boys from downtown. Before I could hide, they spotted me.

The boy on the ground was curled up in a fetal position, his eyes frightened. I was confused—by all rights of geography he should be on the same side as the three big boys. He was from the place we called "Ghost Town," which was at the lower end of the village. The kids from that town were fully Gwich'in. They spoke the language and lived the life.

Standing there, I realized that the boy was on the ground because he was Indian. The three half-breed boys saw him as the enemy, and I was asked to choose sides.

I once had a dream probably inspired by the war movies I'd watched at the showhouse—that Nazi soldiers came to our town to kill us. Before they could plunge a knife into me, I asked them to give me cyanide pills instead. This gut-wrenching nightmare had always haunted me and caused me to wonder if sometime I would be called upon to make such a choice.

When the three boys asked me to choose sides that day, I took the easy way out.

"Kick him," they said, offering me alliance with them.

My foot kicked into the boy's ribs without much impact. He curled. The look in his eyes reminded me of how snared rabbits look when they are about to be choked to death. To this day, I cannot snare rabbits for food without remembering that look.

"You call that a kick?" they asked, proceeding to kick the boy hard. He groaned in agony, and I ran away before they decided the Indian in me needed a good kicking too.

Growing up in Fort Yukon, I never could make sense of this chaos. Just who was the enemy and who was the friend?

When white kids came to our school, we were asked to join forces against them; the poor kids would suffer cruelly at our hands. On some rare occasion an Eskimo child would attend our school, and again there would be fighting. All it took was one kid spouting off racist words and the outsider would receive the brunt of the resulting violence. It did not take many words of hate for your chest to fairly burst with the raw emotion. When it came down to it, I have to admit that there was nothing in any of the kids that we picked on to inspire real hatred. They were nice kids, and many of them would have made good friends.

I don't know how all this got started—only that if there is a mixture of races in a community and a whole lot of ignorance to go along with it, there is sure to be racial discord. We grew up with stories of how the Eskimos had invaded our territory and ruthlessly killed our

My siblings are all smiles in this picture. From left, back row, are Linda, Hannah, Clara, and David in the upper right; in front, from left, are Grafton, Jimmy (sitting on Hannah's lap), and Johnny.

people. Then, when the whites came, they were friendly at first but by the time they began to marry the Native women, they were teaching their children to hate Natives. My mother said that when she visited Fort Yukon as a child, the young half-breed boys called her "squaw." The fighting among the children was reflection of what we had learned. As children we rehearsed the things we heard from the adults around us—mixed with a little James Dean and Marlon Brando, of course.

At home, my mom cocooned and coddled us, but we were on our own the moment we were sent out the front door. The fights made me streetwise. I was not mean-spirited, but I was ready to fight when my younger siblings or I were mistreated. I felt a thrill when I outsmarted my foe. But my ultimate glory, outwitting the Bully, was short-lived. In our teen years he would die from an alcoholic-related sickness. In my adult years I would see how the cycles of negative behavior from our upbringing would determine the patterns our lives would take.

✳ ✳ ✳

When my older siblings went to school in Fort Yukon, there were separate schools— one for the whites, one for the Natives.

My sisters loved telling stories of those days when they had teachers to tease. Once the Bureau of Indian Affairs sent a man and his wife to teach at the Indian school. This couple made no bones about the fact that they hated Indians and they did not want to be in Fort Yukon. He was strict and uppity. Many times he and his wife made the kids stay at their desks after school when they went home for the day. The kids learned to play practical jokes on them.

One time, the teacher asked a couple of students to carry in wood from the woodshed. This was punishment, for he always tried to humble the worst offenders.

Long before this particular teacher's arrival, another teacher was rumored to have killed his wife and burned her body in the school's big furnace. The teacher left town and his wife was never found, leaving the village in suspense; many wondered whether her ghost roamed the schoolhouse and its outbuildings.

So, when they were told to bring firewood from the shed, the kids decided to hide instead. When they did not return, the teacher went to get them. He entered the woodshed and the kids, who were hiding outside, ran to the door and locked him in. They stood listening as their teacher panicked, howling in fright.

Gleefully the kids returned to their desks and proceeded to look innocent. When the maintenance man let the teacher out, the teacher held himself up in dignity and never made mention of the matter again. But he kept up his cranky disposition toward the kids, and they kept up their pranks.

Then there was the time when the teacher and his wife decided to take a break from the village and visit Fairbanks for the weekend. They told everyone about their planned getaway and after school went home to collect their luggage. A group of kids, including my sisters, were walking home past the teacher's cabin. Seeing the open padlock on the hasp, they crept up to the door, put the padlock on, and closed it. Then they ran home and forgot all about it.

Back then most cabins had no backdoor, only small rectangular air holes cut out of the back wall. Except for the two windows that usually graced the cabin, the front door was the only way out.

All their co-workers in the village thought the teacher and his wife were in Fairbanks that weekend, so no one went near their cabin. It wasn't until the following Monday, when they did not show up at work, that a co-worker checked up on them. They had been locked inside the cabin the whole weekend.

The children knew that their horrible prank had gone too far. They snickered in private, for if the culprits were found out they would receive serious reprimands. In the years that followed there were more pranks, and the culprits grin with glee today remembering.

$$* * *$$

My first experiences with schoolteachers were not much better. In first and second grade, my teachers were women who were disciplinarians and took it upon themselves to whip us anytime we so much as looked at them the wrong way. My older brother Jimmy said that having their husbands for teachers was even worse, for the men seemed to take pleasure in spanking the boys.

Once, when my first-grade teacher paddled my behind with a Ping-Pong paddle, I laughed at the foolishness of it. She was a frail thing, in high heels and a skirt, who wore herself out spanking a bunch of us, and it was obvious she was getting tired. When at last she started on me, I started to giggle. She became so incensed that she threw me into the closet for an hour.

Already in the closet was a boy who stank from lack of washing. The other kids sniggered to think of me sharing the closet with this boy whom we called "Flower" after the skunk in Walt Disney's *Bambi*. He did have a powerful smell, but more than that I remember peeking out of the cracks in the closet door and thinking that my teacher was a witch. My first-grade mind conjured up methods of exposing her to be beheaded for her evil ways.

My second-grade teacher was a devil in disguise. She and I locked horns the minute we met. She wrote a note to my father about my attitude. Thinking that my father would shrug it off, as he usually did, I took the note to him.

The next morning, he handed me his note to the teacher.

"Your teacher asked my permission to spank you when she has to, and I told her she has my support," he said, as if validated for all the times he had spanked me.

I managed to keep a low profile that year, but nonetheless the teacher held me back for a couple weeks the following fall. Somehow she felt that I would benefit from being humiliated. The day she graduated me from the second grade to third in mid-semester, she made me push my desk all the way down the hallway to the third-grade classroom while my peers called me a dummy. The teacher did nothing to stop the jeers as I pushed my heavy desk.

I was well acquainted with feelings of rebellion and hatred toward educators when I met my third-grade teacher. She would be the one to open doors in my mind and to restore some of my self-esteem.

Miss McMullin was a black woman. She wore musky perfume, pearly necklaces, and colorful muslin, satin, and embroidered outfits with coordinated shoes to match. In contrast to our mothers—the worn-out souls who cooked for us, washed our clothes, cleaned all day, and took care of our younger siblings while we were at school—Miss McMullin seemed filled with patience, love, and humor. We gravitated toward her. Her accepting nature made us better people. She healed my otherwise tattered soul. In her class, there was room to think; she acknowledged our individuality, and we soaked up this treatment with relish and strove to please her.

Yet kids will always be kids despite the presence of adults, and they will have their own universe. It was during Miss McMullin's time that the Bully was at his most aggressive. For all Miss McMullin's beauty, she never saw the Bully picking on us weaker ones. He made sure of that. He had a smile for her, and when she looked away he had a wet fist and a malicious grin for us.

I never told Miss McMullin. I don't know why. Perhaps I figured that if my father refused to help and told me to fight my own battles, what could a teacher do? I managed to survive the bullies without any help from adults—except for one time.

Each Halloween, we would make masks out of any rudimentary material we could get our hands on. Most of the time it was the big brown paper bags we got from the store. As we trick-or-treated, the bags became so soggy from our cold breath that they would disintegrate. But we were determined to get our fair share of candy.

One year, my older sisters got in the mood to make our masks. Mine was made out of a five-pound cloth sugar sack. My sisters gave it two pointy ears and whiskers. Then, to our delight, they took it upon themselves to take us trick-or-treating.

There was an older guy who had served time in jail, but was still childish enough to want our candy. In the dark of the night, he ran by us and grabbed my bag filled with treats.

My scream must have filled the night, and in a flash my sister Clara went after him. My sisters were tough; they had to be, having grown up wrestling with my older brothers and their friends.

Most of the women in town would have hesitated to give chase because of the man's reputation, but Clara came back moments later with the bag of candy. The assailant lay moaning on the ground. That is the only memory that I have of being protected, and it was a proud moment.

CHAPTER NINE
Life in the Sixties

*T*he Air Force station was a mile above our village. As a child, I was most aware of the military presence at Christmas, for then Santa would be sent down to our school on a dog sled to give out candy and gifts. One time the Air Force sent down a black Santa. None of the children wanted to sit on his lap, for we all knew that Santa was white.

During breakup every year, when the ice broke up on the rivers, signaling the coming of spring, the melting of the snow revealed a winter's worth of paper, cans, and dog poop littering the village. Lake-like puddles and patches of slimy mud appeared, and the stench of untreated waste permeated the village, tempered only by the smell of soggy sawdust and the icy breeze that blew in from the thawing snow. It was then that clean-cut Air Force boys would come down in big blue dump trucks to haul our garbage to the local dump.

The air was filled with excitement when these aliens from another world visited ours. We would peek out from behind the house to catch a glimpse of these men, and they would smile or wink, and we were thrown into fits of giggles. The teenage girls dressed up in their finest clothes and walked about as if they took a promenade each day amidst the mud puddles and the trash.

For the annual Fourth of July celebration, men from the Air Force station would dress up like clowns and join our parade. We kids knew they were generous, so we lined up along the parade route to pick up the wrapped pieces of butterscotch and root beer-flavored hard candy they threw to the crowd.

Years after that I began to understand that the Air Force also contributed to Fort Yukon's nightlife. The air men stationed at the base must have felt like they had been sent to the far side of the moon, and from time to time they would seek out the company of the village women. The men of the village were always fighting to hold the interest of the local women, who often preferred the handsome outsiders to the drudgery of village men and village life. As alcohol became more prevalent in our community, the relationship between the Air Force and the village was filled with tension. I grew up hearing stories of fights between the locals and the enlisted men at the station's nightclub, which after a while came to be nicknamed the "Hug and Slug."

One of the few other forms of entertainment available was AFRN, the radio station from Elmendorf Air Force Base just outside Anchorage. The signal was rebroadcast in Fort Yukon, serving as the village jukebox and our only connection to the outside world. We were raised on its country music and rock-and-roll. Only when the North American Sled Dog Championships were held in Fairbanks did my father try to tune out the AFRN signal, which overpowered KFAR from Fairbanks. He would rig up a long pole connected to a long strand of picture-hanging wire, trying desperately to bring in a clear signal, but the sound of the sportscast always wavered over the great distance.

The rest of the time we were content to listen to the music on AFRN. I enjoyed Wolfman Jack's wild voice and the rock-and-roll he played. In the mornings we awoke to the silliness of the morning disk jockeys. Before we headed out the door to school, we listened to the off-beat humor of the Chicken Man. We always had a wacky sense of humor and this particular show was our favorite.

I often tried to stay awake until eleven o'clock so I could listen to the easy listening instrumentals hosted by disk jockey Pete Smith. He was my favorite, and to be able to stay up for him I had to volunteer to wash dishes at about ten-thirty. I took my time washing each dish and utensil and then proceeded to dry them just as painstakingly. From the back room Jimmy and Martha would peek at me and whisper loudly that I was only doing it to stay up late. I would smile contentedly.

✳ ✳ ✳

Except for our few connections to the outside world—the school, the Air Force station, and its radio station—Fort Yukon was a three-road town. All that broke the quietness was the constant drone of the electrical generator.

By the Yukon River stood the Northern Commercial store with its square facade and wide front porch. Old women and men sat on the porch under the wooden awning, watching the river and the people go by, while young people visited on the steps. We kids hung out on the fringes with one aim in mind: getting money to buy candy, pop, or ice cream. We had no shame when it came to bumming money off others, for our sweet tooth could never be satisfied.

Patty, my childhood friend, and I learned early to hustle for candy. Once we even worked for a quarter, picking up candy wrappers, pop cans, and cigarette butts. We ran over to the NC store, where the big candy bars like Bit O' Honey, Big Hunk, and Oh Henry! sold for three for a quarter.

Our parents never encouraged us to keep our teeth clean other than buy toothpaste and leave it on the shelf. But when the dentist came to town on his annual visit, we sure wished that we had taken better care of our teeth.

As the dentist stuffed a thick cotton lining along our gums and gave us a shot or two with a needle that seemed made of stainless steel, we squirmed and squealed as tears drained from our eyes. The dental assistant suctioned with a serious and unsympathetic look in her eyes.

When at last we were set free, our numbed mouths felt like they hung down to our feet as we staggered out of the room, past a long line of children who waited in death-like fear.

✳ ✳ ✳

In those days, my parents worked hard. My father trapped in the winter. He would load up his toboggan with traps, his gun, and store-bought food, and he would disappear down the road with his team of dogs. My older brothers could not go with him, for they had to attend school. When my father returned home days or weeks later, we younger ones would fight over who pulled off his canvas boots, which were still frozen with ice from the overflow that he had crossed. In winter, even in fifty-below temperatures, sometimes the ice will crack on frozen lakes and rivers, and water will seep through.

After my father had warmed up, we children would take a flashlight and go out to his toboggan and unwrap the frozen string that tied everything down, to see what furs he had trapped. There were frozen lynx, marten, mink, and fox, but we were interested only in the weasels. My father let us have those, and we sold the skins to the store for fifty cents apiece, which equaled six candy bars.

After the animals thawed behind the woodstove on the floor, my parents would roll up their sleeves and sharpen their skinning knives. Wooden stretchers of all sizes would be brought into the house from the cache and every night for almost a week my mother and father carefully skinned each animal. They had to make sure each fur was well tended or the storekeeper would not buy them. These animal skins were the livelihood of our family. The money they brought in allowed us to buy food, electricity, and other items necessary to raise thirteen children.

Once my father took a candle and held its smoking end, slightly tilted, near the mink fur he was tending. He had a gleeful smile upon his face as he brushed the fur, watching the black smoke darken it. This was a way of fooling a buyer into thinking that the fur was more beautiful than it was. We knew this was cheating, but we smiled along with our father.

While my father trapped, my mother cared for our house. She was the jack of all trades within our two-room cabin. She cooked, cleaned, and cared for us all. The older siblings helped her when they could.

At night, after she put us younger ones down to sleep, she would dig out her sewing. She was always working on something. If she was not sewing our boots, parkas, and clothes, she worked on items to sell to the teachers, nurses, and Air Force men who lived temporarily in our village. Many nights my mother spent carefully sewing Indian dolls complete with fur parkas and boots. She used old socks to stuff the dolls, for she had nothing else. Today she laughs that somewhere out there in the world are handmade dolls filled with our old socks.

We helped our mother whenever she asked. We fought over who would scrape baby "dah" off the sodden diapers with a table knife. We also proved helpful when my mother prepared to sell her home-brew. We washed the green wine bottles in a big tub. As the stuff brewed in its yeasty scent behind the stove, we lined up and took turns dipping the ladle into the barrel for a taste. My mother was irate at the time, but later I heard her laughing about it with some adult. My mother and father tried bootlegging, but like others who tried they always ended up being their own best customers.

* * *

Every fall, my older brothers gathered dried goose grass from along the lake for bedding for the sled dogs. From August until mid-September, my parents cut and hung the dog salmon that they caught

Two younger Wallis boys checking the fish wheel at our camp down river.

in the fish wheel for their winter supply of dog food. We helped by keeping out of the way and demanding little of their time.

With all this activity going on, the dogs lolled in the yard all summer. We hardly noticed them—they were workers, not pets. They seemed to know their status in life and treated us children with contempt, snapping their eyes at us, or yawning in boredom as they watched us play. Just before snowfall, the dogs would perk up, knowing their time in the harness was approaching.

My older brothers cooked the dog food in a huge blackened container on the fireplace outside. They put cut-up pieces of fish, water, and God knows what else into that pot. All through the afternoon, the food would cook and simmer. At night, long after supper and just before bedtime, we younger ones had to find a way to get the dog pots away from the dogs to feed them. The pots were whatever my father could get his hands on: coffee cans, basins, cooking pans. They were bent and beat up by the aggressive chewing, and with a long stick we managed to collect them. Then we would carefully dunk a coffee can into the dog food and scoop it out, evenly portioning it out to the more than a dozen barking, hungry dogs.

Whatever had been put into the dog pot, it smelled horrible. When one of us was unlucky enough to get it on our gloves, the stench was hard to get out.

I was afraid of the dogs. Some of my older brothers cuddled the dogs but I never had the nerve, for most were bigger than I was. I played with the puppies. The bigger dogs always seemed famished, and some had husky or wolf in them. When it was time to feed them, we practically threw their pots to them as they strained ferociously against their tethers. I had nightmares about wolf dogs trying to eat me.

Before winter set in, my father took his older sons out into the woods with his boat and they would gather more than seventeen cords of wood. My brothers cut, chopped, and stacked the wood, enough to heat two stoves all winter, with no shortage. The wood would cover one end of our yard right up to the front window. We younger ones loved playing on the woodpile. My mother warned us of the danger of falling off, but when she looked away we were climbing again.

In addition to tending the woodpile, the older boys had to keep our fifty-gallon galvanized water barrel filled. The rule was that the barrel had to be filled high enough that we little ones could dip out water. When the water level sank below our reach, the older brothers had to fill the barrel again.

Occasionally the water level would get down to the bottom. Once Barry and I felt we were dying of thirst as we stretched down trying to get some water. He heaved himself over the edge and tried to scoop water into the dipper. He lost control and found himself falling toward the foot of water at the bottom of the barrel. I screamed and tried to hold onto his feet. But he caught himself with his hands on the inner sides of the barrel and slowly inched himself back up. Our mother had to be dragged away from her work to help extract him.

To fill the water barrel, the older brother had to haul water from a hole chopped into the thick ice on the Yukon River. The water hole was chopped into the ice using an ax and a chisel. People from the village cooperated in keeping the hole open. Sometimes they kept it from freezing over by covering it with cardboard or canvas. Other times they tossed handfuls of clean snow into the water, and that kept the hole from freezing up. It was considered a minor crime to allow the water hole to freeze up.

We younger siblings sometimes helped the older boys push the sled laden with water buckets up the small hill to our house. The buckets were made out of square five-gallon Chevron gas cans. The gas smell was burnt out of the cans, which were then washed with soapy water, and carried by handles woven out of baling wire. The water jostled around and splashed us if we were not careful.

Every day or two, all year long, the water tank had to be filled if we wanted water to cook and clean with, and to drink. Villagers who packed water for wages made a good living, especially in the summer when the buckets of water had to be carted on a handmade wheelbarrow.

Our neighbor "Pa"Williams packed water for a living. People went to his house and let him know that they needed their barrels filled. It cost from three to five dollars, depending on how far he had to haul the water. When the men of our family were too busy, my mother would depend on Pa to pack our water. Others packed water, but most people preferred Pa because of his lively sense of humor. After filling the barrels, he would linger to fill his customers in on the village news.

In the spring, we looked forward to the returning sun and its heat that melted everything until the leaves let go of their fragrance and it filled the air. My siblings and I fought like dogs over the muskrat tails that we toasted on top of the woodstove until they were crisp and tasted like pork rinds, only better. Beaver meat was delicious, too, with its willowy flavor, and we devoured the boiled meat with relish. But there was no comparison to the singed duck soup that my mother made with dried vegetable flakes, adding rice and macaroni. We always ate our duck soup with Pilot Boy crackers spread with margarine. These foods were all we knew, and to this day, I can't say I know of a finer meal.

Summer arrived with its long, languid days. The mosquitoes came alive, and soon the flying ants landed. Then came the pincher bugs we called antennae bugs, followed by the horseflies that bit into our flesh. At the end of summer, the gnats came, as the days got cooler

Barry, me, and Becky. We found ways to play in all seasons but especially loved the long, languid days of summer.

and the stars above could be seen even before it was truly dark. Our summers were heralded in and out by these bugs, who made their presence known in great numbers. Every now and again we would get our hands on some "bug dope" to repel them, but the rest of the time we tolerated them without giving it much thought.

At the end of June and in early July, my parents caught, cut, and dried the huge salmon that swam up the Yukon to their spawning grounds. My mother would be completely oblivious to the bees and flies that tried to get at the fish as she expertly cut them to hang in our cache behind the house.

The big salmon hung low from the high racks. We children would sneak into the cache when no one was around and eat off the bottom of the hanging fish. It mattered little whether the fish was raw or dry. We devoured the meat, and when my mother caught us she scowled, telling us we were no better than the camp-robbers, the gray jays that hung around caches to steal meat.

✳ ✳ ✳

In these times of our village life, there were long periods of peace, but in between there was conflict and violence. I remember coming home from school one Christmas, all happy and filled with hope, but as I drew closer to our house I could smell the home-brew. I knew then that we children were in for one long holiday.

The adults of Fort Yukon always had good intentions. They wanted to take time off from all their hard work and from raising their many children, but they never seemed to resolve the issues in their lives when they were sober. When they drank, all those issues came out in the form of tears, blows, and harsh words.

Throughout the year people drank occasionally, but most of the drinking took place during Christmastime or the Fourth of July. We children expected the holiday drinking but we were promised a happy time.

My father would order new clothes for us and give us haircuts, while my mother made us brand-new canvas boots. The tree was put up, and the adults were heard whispering, filling us little ones with excitement. All the while the home-brew was slowly concocting in the wooden barrel. The scent filled our noses, vaguely warning us that the happiness would not come.

On Christmas Eve we were put to bed. None of us could sleep for the air was always filled with tension, exciting yet foreboding. Friends would arrive, and my father would generously pop open the first bottle of home-brew. Everyone would toast the season and take their first drink. We children would peek from out from the back room. We watched our parents laughing and telling stories with their friends. We noted that the older siblings always disappeared during these times. We could not sleep as the noise got louder.

Before midnight, and with half a dozen empty green bottles littering the table, the happy adults began to cry. Then their tears would dry up into angry words, and before anyone could redirect the party, it would erupt into anger. My father would end up tossing people out of his house left and right.

About this time my parents would start fighting. Jimmy, Martha, the younger siblings, and I all witnessed my father beat my mother with his fists.

It was unfathomable to us why my mother would not back down. One moment she was lying in a heap on the floor, but as soon as she recovered she was like Muhammad Ali, bouncing back up and challenging my father all over again.

"Hit me again, Pete!" she taunted him over and over.

Then we children would try to intervene. We begged our father to stop hitting our mother, and we pleaded with our mother to stop telling him to hit her again. But they were in their own world and did not even notice us.

After days of drinking and fighting came the slow, painful task of sobering up. My mother's swollen face would gradually heal. My father's face would go blank as if nothing had happened. There was an emptiness about our cabin as in the aftermath of war—a war no one had won.

Slowly the stove became warm again, food smells filled the air, the older siblings trickled back to the cabin, and we began to cheer up. Life returned to normal. My father would pretend to forget that he had beaten the woman who had given him thirteen children, and she would pretend to forgive him. We had to pretend, too—pretend that we had not witnessed anything out of the ordinary. It was a neat little trick, one that we performed again and again.

Once, my mother looked out the window at us playing in the yard and saw us reenact their fights. No one wanted to be Mom, but everyone wanted to be Daddy. The rest of us played our parts, crying, "Daddy! Daddy! Don't hit Momma!"

My mother ran out of the house. She had an urgency about her, as if she did not want this rude reminder of those times she so desperately wanted to forget. We went running in different directions, for she had caught us playing the forbidden game of "Hit me again, Pete!"

✳ ✳ ✳

In sobriety, my parents' relationship was strange. They were like business partners who happened to have children together and each intended to contribute a fair share to raising them. They worked well side by side, cutting fish or moose meat, or preparing other Native foods. While he trapped and worked outdoors, she kept everything in working order at home. But they rarely showed any sign of affection for each other.

At times, they would sit at the table and talk with each other laughingly. We played contentedly by their feet. Some part of us knew the other story to be real in its ugliness, but for the sake of our parents we played along with this fairy tale, knowing it would not last. We loved our parents when they were sober but detested them when they drank. The drinking patterns were so predictable that we automatically treated them with disrespect during those times.

This part of our life together was always there. As much as we hoped the drinking would go away, it was interwoven into our lives. When it wasn't our parents being disruptive, it was our neighbors or a friend's parents. We watched sadly from a distance as a man chased his wife down the road. My heart would cry for the woman when she was caught.

A painting by Andrew Wyeth appeared in one of my schoolbooks. This picture always stuck in my memory, showing a slender woman in a mustard-colored dress sitting in some dry, wheat-colored grass. She seemed to be hiding from a nearby house. I imagined her to be one of the abused wives. In my mind I hid with her and hoped for her safety.

I referred to the periods of drinking as the dark days and the periods of sobriety as the sunny days. Many times Barry and I sought solace from the violence of our drunken parents by pretending we were the children of a man and woman whose faces we had cut out of a wig advertisement. They were a handsome couple. Barry and I would lie in our beds holding the cut-outs as they smiled lovingly back at us. In the front room of our cabin, our parents drank. We never told anyone of our fantasy, for it would have seemed disloyal to our parents, who were good people when they were sober.

✳ ✳ ✳

I did not know it then, but my mother had not started drinking until 1964, when my brother Grafton was killed in an accident with a truck.

Grafton was a born imp who loved to tease and play. The morning of the accident, he had teased his sisters relentlessly before school. He threw them in the snow and pulled their hair, so they ran back to the house to complain about him. Grafton kept running back into the house for dry gloves, for he kept getting his wet. Because he was teasing his sisters, my mother told him to get out and not to come back again as she handed him his third pair of gloves. Those words would ring in her head for years to come.

Completely unabashed by his mother's words, Grafton gleefully ran out of the house and off to school. On his way, he spotted the clinic's water tank being pulled by a truck. The driver, a responsible person, always kept an eye out for the mischievous kids who tried to grab the truck's back fender and get a free slide on the ice. That day he did not see Grafton behind him sliding along the ice. When the driver backed up the truck, my brother was crushed.

After Grafton died, my father was full of blame. He wanted to kill the driver. My mother sank into her own oblivion. Both parents slunk off into their dark little corners. They could find no relief from their grief over this special son.

My mother sought refuge in liquor. My father, who always drank, found one more reason to do so as he sat for hours crying. When they sobered, the pain was still there, but they faced the daily drudgery of their lives stoically until the next alcoholic episode.

I was too young to remember Grafton. But when my parents drank they cried unceasingly over his memory, and this made me sad. To this day when I am around those who drink into the night when the tears and sorrow come, I feel an indescribable pain.

✳ ✳ ✳

In the late sixties, my father was diagnosed with diabetes. He was forced to quit drinking. When he quit drinking, so did my mother. But Itchoo still drank.

On the first of the month when the welfare checks came in the mail, people would scurry to pay their bills at the store and at the utilities company, and then they sought out the bootleggers. After she had consumed the bootleggers' wares, Itchoo would come stumbling into our yard wearing her long dress and a scarf wrapped around her head like a turban, with a cane in one hand, either singing a song or cussing up a storm. A dark cloud of rage would come over

Becky learns how to clean salmon. We all shared in the chores.

my father's face and he would send my mother out to contend with taking Grandma home to bed.

Itchoo and my father understood each other too well. Many times we saw the tightening of his lips when she summoned him, and we heard his complaints about "those people uptown" who made her drink.

For many years, Itchoo lived in a small house by the river near Aunt Nina. I visited that house once when my brother Brady was born. Midwives had piled into the front room of our cabin. There was Nina Flitt, the local midwife, and Olive Solomon, the trained nurse, and a couple other women who would aid my mother in the birthing of her twelfth child.

My younger siblings and I tittered about nervously, not understanding what all the whispering and the preparations were about. In the nine months that my mother had been pregnant, we had not noticed. She had not altered her chore routine at all, nor did her weight seem to change. She was always round. She once said that it was years before she could see her feet again.

The midwives puttered about silently in the sacred ceremony of childbirth. We became frantic as they pinned a couple of bedsheets around the big white bed from the Hudson Stuck Memorial Hospital, one of which could be found in just about every cabin in Fort Yukon after the auction years before.

The midwives commanded my older siblings to take us down to our grandmother's house by the river. We were hesitant, for we feared our mother's life was in danger. Nonetheless, we were taken almost by force to Itchoo's.

In the gray daylight of the February day, we sat by the table next to the window, watching Itchoo placidly cooking biscuits in her skillet pan atop a potbellied aluminum stove that blazed hot and even. From her homemade hutch Itchoo took down porcelain cups, placed them on rose-bordered saucers, and poured into them mahogany-colored tea. As we sat chewing on buttered biscuits and drinking hot, sugared tea from delicate cups, our wide eyes took in the many mysteries of our grandmother's domain.

Her small cabin had no back door, only a screened front door and three windows, two long ones on the side and one small one on the front. Inside, colorful fabric hung along ropes to serve as walls for her bedroom. The chamber pot, typically kept behind the front door in the winter, was hidden in her bedroom.

That would be the last time we had a privileged glimpse into the life of the woman who would remain forever a mystery to us.

∗ ∗ ∗

Itchoo was the cause of recurrent argument between Aunt Nina and my father over who should take care of her. In her old age, she could hardly move around. She was partially blind, for she had contracted a virus that had resulted in the loss of one eye. In its place she wore a blue glass eye, and she could hardly see out of the remaining eye.

Given the choice, my grandmother chose the offspring who offered her the best treatment at the time. After living near my Aunt Nina, Itchoo one day moved into a cabin next to ours.

Itchoo seemed close to our older siblings. Despite the fact that the older ones did not speak Gwich'in any more than we could, they had a rapport with Itchoo that we younger ones were not able to establish. We never knew that Itchoo had lived in a different culture before the coming of the Western culture, and no one thought to explain this to us.

While my grandmother doted on my older siblings, she was a harsh stranger to us. In general we kept our distance. As children we tried hard to please her, sometimes being brave enough to approach her for treats or some token of her love. Sometimes she surprised us by giving us money, candy, or a friendly smile. More often we were perplexed by this woman and her blue glass eye, and we would peek at her only to be shooed away when she caught us.

At times when my older siblings were off doing their own thing, my mother would ask one of us younger ones to spend the night with Itchoo. Sometimes Martha and Jimmy would do it, but occasionally I was selected, and my heart would do little frightened flip-flops at the thought of spending a night alone with my strange grandmother. I would beg Barry to accompany me, and he would do so reluctantly.

Aside from being taught how to be devout by the Episcopal Church, Itchoo was very superstitious. She said Barry would one day be a medicine man, and for some reason she was never comfortable in his presence. But I would be there and she did not fear me.

Before Itchoo went to sleep, she would take out her blue glass eye and set it on her bedside table. Then she would perform various other bedtime rituals, fluffing up her pillow and rearranging her bedclothes. Finally she began to pray.

Barry and I peeked at her from under our covers. We could hear the word *Nagwathut*, which means God. Just when it sounded as if she had finished her prayers and we would be able to go to sleep, she would remember one more person she had forgotten. Eventually, her prayers would end and then we would lie awake, listening to her snore and dream out loud.

CHAPTER TEN
Times of Change

*T*he year 1968 brought the first of several unexpected changes for my family. That hot, sultry summer, a bigger airport was being built in Chalkyitsik. The men who razed the brush and trees accidentally let the blaze get out of hand, and the fire roared toward Fort Yukon. Firefighters worked hard to squelch the flames that were aided and abetted by the hot weather.

As children, we were unaffected by the stress that the adults suffered, worrying about the impending destruction of the winter traplines between Chalkyitsik and Fort Yukon that were their livelihood. To my eight-year-old senses, the smoke from a wildfire was just one of the many smells of summer.

Itchoo was beside herself. *Neegoogwandah* was her hunting and trapping land. She was terribly ill, and the stress of knowing that her beloved lands were going to burn made her sicker. Speaking in Gwich'in, she begged my father to do something.

He frowned, telling her there was nothing he could do.

Frantically, she asked him to take his older sons up to her land and build a firebreak around it.

My father remained detached. "It's up to the BLM to put the fires out! They have plenty of firefighters up there now!" he said, scowling at his mother.

My father worked at the generator house and did not want to leave his job, especially since the Bureau of Land Management was paying many other men good wages to fight the fire.

I asked my mother, "Mama, why is Itchoo trying to save that land?"

My mother usually did not allow us to ask questions. It made life easier if questions did not have to be answered. But on that day she may have needed to talk to someone, for she could not do so with my father.

"Years ago, in her youth, Itchoo planted a tree," my mother explained. "There was an old Gwich'in belief that if she tended and cared for the tree throughout her life, she would live as long as that tree lived."

"Do you mean if the tree burns down, she will die?" I asked in disbelief.

My mother nodded her head sadly. I prayed frantically that my father would rush up to the land and save the tree. For the first time I began to sense the futility that my parents fell victim to.

We lived directly under the flight path of the planes coming in to land at the airport, and as children we always dared one another to stand on top of the roof until a big BLM plane flew overhead. Usually we chickened out and climbed off the roof. One time I slipped and began sliding off the roof. Martha and Jimmy encouraged me to jump as I hung from the edge by my fingers. I looked down and saw the ground far below. Determined not to fall and break my legs, I managed to climb back up.

Now I imagined that my father and grandmother were feeling some of the same things I had felt when I had been hanging from the roof. I wondered if they could save themselves with a little effort.

My mother tried to get my father to save Itchoo's tree and the trapping lands that our family depended on, but his scowl only deepened. Soon my mother had to accept that the situation was out of her hands.

The next morning, when my mother went to take Itchoo her breakfast, she found my grandmother's house a mess. Her Bible lay open on the floor, and papers and other personal items were strewn about as if blown by a small whirlwind. My grandmother lay there, breathing but unresponsive.

The hot summer day was quiet as women and men from all over town came down to pay Martha Wallis their last respects. We children were forbidden to go near Itchoo's cabin. I shuffled my feet in the dirt outside as I hovered nearby, trying to catch a glimpse of something I could understand. The stoic manner of all the adults gave me the sense that all this was beyond me.

My other siblings stayed inside the house, obeying my mother's wishes, while I stood outside watching people silently come and go all day long. I wanted to understand the mystery. A part of me knew that Itchoo was going to die, but I had not yet experienced a human death—or at least not one I could remember—so I did not believe it would happen to Itchoo. She had such a powerful presence that I could not imagine her leaving this world.

Sometime in the late afternoon, I looked up to the sky and felt a sudden change in the atmosphere. Whereas the past few days had been hot and unrelentingly dry, now soft moisture filled the air. From

My mom and me during her drinking years.

across the Yukon River a deep rainbow appeared, and soft drops fell upon my upturned face. I knew a change had occurred.

It wasn't long before my mother passed by me, weeping. She paused long enough to tell me that Itchoo was no longer with us.

I don't remember much about Itchoo's funeral, but later when my parents had been drinking their home-brew, my mother would accuse my father of allowing Itchoo to die by not saving her tree. My father would weep but found no consolation.

It was that way with my mother and father. Where she faithfully believed all that she had been raised to believe and came to understanding along the way, my father questioned every faith and found no end to his confusion. He had been taught to believe in God who had created us all, yet my father had lost his first wife and many loved ones, and in those dark times he saw no evidence of a kind God. Yet he was still told to worship, obey, and believe. On the other side he also had been raised on Shamanism, a belief that some people condemned as witchcraft. He stated many times that he would not believe in any religion proclaimed by human beings until he saw proof of it with his own eyes.

✳ ✳ ✳

More changes were to come. My older sister Clara fell in love with one of the men from the Air Force station and in time traveled to Michigan to marry him. My father hid his sorrow with a scowl, but after she left he expressed his grief by going through a long period of depression.

My eldest sister, Hannah, was beautiful beyond words, but her manner was that of my grandmother Martha Itchoo, who lived life her own way. Whenever anyone tried to set her straight, she immediately went in the opposite direction.

Against the wishes of my father, Hannah eloped with a handsome Hun Gwich'in named Tony Paul from the village of Eagle, Alaska. They made an attractive couple, and it took my father some time to warm up to the man who had married his treasured daughter.

My third sister, Linda, also was born with her own mind. She married a man whom my father disapproved of, but eventually he softened, especially after his grandson Bobby was born.

Itchoo had left the spirit of independence in all the female members of our family.

✳ ✳ ✳

The impact of the outside world came by way of mail to Fort Yukon in 1970. Papers were sent to all the villagers, telling of proposed allotments and land that in the future would be owned by corporations. Many of the people from our village were confused by this idea. How could they be asked to "select" land that they had used for thousands of years?

My grandmother and my father took for granted that Neegoogwandah was theirs to use for hunting and trapping. This was the Gwich'in way. There were no papers, no bills of sale. People knew who used certain lands, and out of respect no one trespassed.

One time, my father and my uncle Tim went to their spring trapping lands and found two men sitting on the very spot where they had always camped in the spring. Before the white man came, such an act would have incited a tribal war. But these were relatively modern days, and murder was seen as a sin in the new eyes of the Gwich'in.

Instead of killing the men, Uncle Tim unceremoniously kicked the teapot on their campfire high into the air. Then he stomped out the flames with his boots, his eyes never flinching from the quiet men.

Without further incident, the men packed their gear and left. They had gambled that the Wallis brothers were not up to trapping that year, and it was a gamble they lost.

* * *

When my father received shares in the Doyon Native Corporation, he was flabbergasted that all of Alaska's Interior Native lands had been lumped together into one Native corporation that would be headquartered in Fairbanks. As he read the explanations, he was not comfortable with the fact that lands near his trapping lands were being put into the hands of a smaller local corporation. Whatever was not allotted for personal use would be put under the control of the larger corporation based in Fairbanks.

I listened to his interpretation of this new issue as he explained it to my mother and gave his opinion.

"That means someone way downriver will have equal shares of our land up here, and we will have the same ownership of their lands. If the Corporation messes up, then the IRS or any other agency that the Corporation owes money to can claim these lands. Our lands."

My father went on and on. My mother listened as she shuffled the parchment-like paper that the Doyon Corporation had sent to all the villages. My father rebuked the idea. The concept of owning stock in tribal lands was unacceptable to him. My father was like a stone that was hard to carve.

My mother, on the other hand, was always open to new ideas and ways of life. She picked up the stock certificates from where my father had tossed them carelessly and put them into her box of important papers, where they have remained.

Not only was my father not ready for the changes that were to come our way, but he was downright hostile about them. Seeing his face was like watching a storm cloud gather force.

When a woman came to sign my family up for welfare, my father turned her out. This upset my mother. She knew that everyone Uptown was applying for the government's handouts, and she knew that my father was not well enough to continue supporting us. But she kept her silence, knowing her objections would only deepen my father's scowl.

CHAPTER ELEVEN

Turning Points

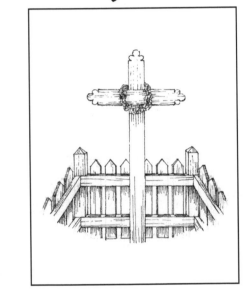

*I*n July of 1972, cousin Kay came to visit us. She was the daughter of my father's brother, Tim, who had moved to Fairbanks in the 1960s. She had been attending school outside Alaska for years. We were used to seeing Uncle Tim's eldest son, also named Tim, for he lived in Fairbanks and came to visit us occasionally. But the only image we had of Kay came from a beautiful eight-by-ten black-and-white photograph of her posing in a crown.

I could not believe anyone that beautiful could be related to us, and I spent hours staring at her picture, imagining her to be a fairy queen from another land. When I heard she was coming to Fort Yukon, I could hardly contain my excitement—I finally would meet the queen from the black-and-white glossy.

I was not the only one excited. It had been years since my father had seen his niece. His brother Tim had long since died in Fairbanks, and my father eagerly anticipated seeing Tim's daughter.

After my father was diagnosed with diabetes, he had been told to eat fresh vegetables, and the freshest ones available in the village came in cans. For Kay, he dug into his health food larder for canned corn, canned asparagus, and canned peaches to be served with fresh salmon for the feast in her honor.

When Kay arrived, we younger ones were like shy puppies. She turned out to be a kind, loving person who wanted to embrace all of us at once.

My father was almost possessive of Kay. We stood by as he beamed with pride at his beautiful niece who not only had succeeded in the outside world but was also on her way to a secondary education.

Kay's visit would mark the time when we as villagers began to shed our skins of innocence to the outside world.

After Kay's visit, her older sister Ruth arrived. We were in awe of her, for she had an air of sophistication that defied us and defeated my father. Unlike Kay's soft and loving look, Ruth was very matter-of-fact. She would look my father square in the eye and not flinch. My father had not known a woman of such caliber since his own mother had passed away.

My father was never to know that most women from the villages would follow the example of Ruth, by being stronger than the men around

Grandma Martha Itchoo, left, and Auntie Nina in 1968.

them. He could never be comfortable with such women, for they were a stark reminder of his own mother—fiercely independent by nature and able to meet the world head-on.

✳ ✳ ✳

When Ruth returned to Fairbanks to spend more time with her brother Tim and his family before returning to her home in Seattle, my father got on the plane with her. He had an appointment for a medical check-up in Fairbanks.

Days later when he returned we were in for a shock. He had broken his long spell of sobriety by bringing home cases of whiskey. He was half-drunk and smiled jovially.

To explain falling off the wagon, he told my mother that the doctor had found a cyst that would have to be removed surgically. He knew his medical problem could be solved, but he had waited too long for death to take him in this life he had lived seemingly over and over, with no end. Now, he would turn to the only medicine he knew to cure his pain and sorrow: alcohol. If death would not take him, then he would go to death.

About the same time, Social Security benefits arrived, and my father received a huge amount of money. I was twelve, and the thrill of all that money being available to my family sparked my greediness. I decided that a trip to Fairbanks for Barry and me would be a better use for the money than my father wasting it on whiskey, so I wrote him a letter appealing to his generosity.

Had not my father been half-drunk and surrounded by his buddies from the village, he would not have been amused by my request to visit Fairbanks. But as his friends laughed at his audacious daughter, my father dug into his pocket and handed me a roll of bills. I don't remember the amount, but it was enough to get round-trip tickets for me, Barry, and my brother Johnny, who came as a chaperone.

As I gleefully rushed out of the house the next day on my way to Fairbanks, my mother frantically pulled me aside and whispered to me to deliver a message to my cousin Tim. My mother knew that my father respected his nephew and might listen to him when he would listen to no one else.

"Tell him that his uncle is trying to kill himself with drink," she said. "Tell him we need his help."

* * *

In Fairbanks we stayed in Hamilton Acres with our cousin Tim and his wife, Mary. At first we thought that the neighborhood was the whole of Fairbanks. Then, when Tim had time off from his job with the Native corporation, he took us sightseeing. We went to Foodland on Gaffney Road, in downtown Fairbanks. Tim pointed out the round architecture of the supermarket, then he took us to the Goldstream Theater, and our eyes would hardly blink for fear of missing anything. Everything we saw impressed us.

Our eyes were drawn to the city folk. When we saw black people, we stared until we realized we were being rude. When we saw fat people in shorts and tank tops, our mouths dropped open. When we saw girls and women wearing tight shorts and halter-tops, our mouths dropped open wider. People with red hair and freckles made us stare. There was nothing that did not shock us. We took it all in.

To the people of Fairbanks, all these sights were daily events. But to our village senses, everything was astonishing—the smells from the delis and restaurants, the great number of people, the way the people dressed, the big-city attitude. The Fairbanksans all seemed so sophisticated I could almost feel my village simpleness like a sheath around my body.

In the evenings, Barry and I would go with the neighborhood kids to put pennies on the railroad tracks nearby. The next morning we collected our smashed coins. These were the only souvenirs we took home.

Our minds had been opened to the reality that beyond the Yukon Flats and over the White Mountains lay a different world. In the years that followed, continually we would be drawn back to Fairbanks, and beyond it.

The time drew near for us to return to Fort Yukon. I had tried to conjure courage to deliver my mother's message to Tim. But I was a shy child and there were so many distractions that ultimately the message went undelivered. Besides, I had seen my father drink like this for most of my life, and he always managed to pull himself out of it.

When we flew back to Fort Yukon, my father was still drinking. He lay drunk and getting meaner by the day on the green Hide-a-Bed that he had proudly purchased a year before. It and our propane stove, electric freezer, and washing machine were signs that our family was moving quickly into the modern world.

My mother was disappointed that I had not delivered her message. After that, she seemed to resign herself to her husband's drinking.

When we awoke in the morning my father lay on his bed drinking. By the time we came home from school, he was morose. He possessed an ornery disposition, and we learned quickly that the only way to avoid his drunken ire was to stay quiet in his presence. No laughing, no talking, only silence would fill the front room of our cabin, month after month, as he lay on his bed sinking deeper into his misery. If we showed signs of life, he became angry and then we would have to sit and listen to him tell us what a waste of space we were. He would threaten to tie us to an oil drum and roll us down a hill. This filled us with terror. It never occurred to us that carrying out this threat would have been too much for him in his weakened state.

He was disappointed in his life, and he found no way to assuage his despair other than to pick on us.

By this time, Jimmy was fourteen, Martha was thirteen, I was twelve, and Barry was eleven. The four of us—the oldest children still in the household—took to staying uptown at Fort Yukon's new community center. It had a laundry room, shower stalls, a library, a gymnasium, and snack machines. The community center was the place where many of the village children gathered to get away from drinking parents or unhappy homes. When bingo and pull-tabs became popular in our village, many bingo orphans would practically live at the center.

I stood at the crossroads between childhood and adulthood, petrified as I watched my father's determined efforts to drink himself to death. All around childhood friends were changing by the minute, being transformed from children to adults, while inside I kept screaming that *the world must not change!*

＊ ＊ ＊

The last autumn of my father's life was hellish. As he became increasingly ill, we tried to go on with our everyday lives while walking on eggshells around him. He spent his most lucid moments trying to find fault with us, and when he caught us doing something wrong we would have to endure hours of lecturing. Eventually he would end up crying drunkenly, and later I would detest any drunk who cried.

Our home life made learning at school difficult. We could not concentrate on what the teachers were saying, nor could we be happy with our friends as we once had been. But out of habit I kept going to school, despite the fact that I was failing. Catching me skipping school would have given my father further reason to be angry with me.

In home economics class, we learned how to bake bread, to make jams and jellies out of rose-hips, and to crochet. I never learned how to cast off the scarf I crocheted, because I had skipped class on that particular day, so I just kept crocheting.

"How long do you intend to crochet that thing?" my father asked one day, in a rare show of curiosity. I shrugged, trying to act like I knew what I was doing. Then he asked me to take the scarf out of the bag, so I did. The scarf stretched all the way from the front room to the back of our cabin. It was one of the few times that fall that everyone in our family laughed. I was glad he did not question me about this, for he might have figured out that I was in the early stages of dropping out of school.

By Christmas, we had come to think of my father as the angry thing in the front room. More and more, we older ones stayed away from home.

About a week after Christmas, my father told me to go to the store and get some oranges. That year the Northern Commercial store had been moved all the way uptown and renamed the Alaska Commercial store. The post office also had moved out of the downtown area. What had once been the hub of Fort Yukon was now a ghost town, and we now lived in a dark place by the river.

Walking uptown through the narrow trails with spruce trees standing tall and stark in the night, with only a few houses between our cabin and Uptown, was no small feat for a girl like me. I was too imaginative, and every dark form I could make out on the one-mile trip uptown frightened me. My heart pounded loudly in my ears and many times I would stop and listen, thinking I heard a suspicious sound.

I did not relish the idea of taking that long walk just so my father could have some oranges. Besides, I was tired of taking his abuse. So I took the only way out. I procrastinated.

This was a definite act of rebellion as far as my father was concerned. "You'd better get going before I tan your hide," he said with a warning look in his eyes. Knowing he was too weak to move, I daringly told him to wait.

My father was enraged. Never before had any of us gone against even the smallest of his commands. But he and I had a sudden realization together—he could not do a damn thing about it.

"When I get better, you will really get it good from me," he said quietly, and I listened as I drank my tea. I knew there was a good possibility that he was right, but it felt so good to do as I pleased for once.

Eventually I gave in and ran like a scared rabbit through the darkness to the store to buy the oranges. When I returned home, I spotted the clinic's blue Suburban parked by our house, and I knew instantly that it had come for my father. As the men carefully hauled my father out on a stretcher he kept his eyes on me. He had always been bulky and not even his sickness had lessened his weight. I heard one of the men comment on how heavy he was, but still my father's eyes were locked onto mine. As much as I wanted to look away as guilt nagged at me, I could not, my fist tight around the bag of oranges.

My mother escorted my father on the medivac flight that night to the Fairbanks hospital. After they had left, my siblings and I turned on both lights in the front room, which hadn't been brightly lit for months. We stripped our father's bed and cleaned the front room. My younger siblings bounced gleefully on the couch.

Barry had been Uptown the whole time, and when he arrived we asked him to guess what had changed. After fifteen minutes of guessing we had to tell him. His eyes fell on the empty couch and realization dawned in his eyes, followed by a deep remorse that he had not noticed our father was gone.

All of us played late into the night. The older siblings were supposed to watch us and peeked in occasionally. We were having quite a time until it suddenly struck me that our father might die.

"You guys be quiet!" I said, feeling sad all of a sudden. "Don't you know Daddy could die!"

My younger brothers quieted down then, and soon we went to sleep in the slightly chilly cabin.

The next morning, on January 4, 1973, we heard that my father had died in the night. We were shocked, but mostly we were numb from the many months that we had spent silenced by his drinking. On his death certificate, it was written that he died of diabetes or some related condition, but we knew better.

CHAPTER TWELVE
Back & Forth

*T*he last remnants of structure in our lives were about to crumble away.

No one told us that my Aunt Nina was giving a potluck at her house, so we took it upon ourselves to provide something for those who attended the funeral. We bought white bread and jars of peanut butter and jelly, and made stacks of sandwiches. After the funeral, everyone packed into our cabin and ate those. Then, I learned later, they gravitated down to my aunt's house to eat. But at the time I felt we had provided good potluck food in my father's honor.

I was the only one who tried to go back to school right after my father's death, but people kept staring at me with a quiet, knowing look, and I felt like such an outsider that I went home. I realized why people go into hiding when a loved one dies.

The funeral was even worse. I felt that people came to the church only to witness our grief, rather than to share in it. Finally I could stand no more, so I left with a friend. She was also staring at me in that funny way, though, so I told her goodbye as well.

I held inside an overwhelming need to weep. Now I know that it is not good to hold grief inside. If I could live that day again, I would behave like the stereotypical Italian grandmother, publicly weeping and gnashing my teeth.

After everything was over and done with, we were left alone in our little world. My sister Martha left home, first moving to Eagle, where my older sister Hannah lived, then traveling to Michigan, where my second-eldest sister, Clara, lived. The older boys were in and out of the house, so it was the younger ones who were left at home with my mother. I knew that my older siblings had lives of their own but as they all trickled away, I felt for the first time an echoing emptiness in our two-room cabin.

As miserable as my father was in his last days, his ornery disposition had kept the family together. While he had occupied the front room, the older boys still cut wood and fed the dogs, my mother cooked and cleaned, and we younger ones helped out when we could. After he died, everyone slacked off.

My older brothers spent their days uptown with their buddies, drinking and listening to songs by Hank Williams Sr. and other country music that people loved to listen to as they drank.

My mother, who had always been our quiet, dependable care-taker, withdrew further into depression. She had not been on her own since she was sixteen, and the responsibilities before her were over-whelming. It seemed after my father died that a part of her died too, for she became quiet and faded into the background.

Each night I listened to her cry softly. One night our eyes met and the grief that I saw was something I did not know how to alleviate, so I looked away.

Soon after, my mother snuck away to have her first drink after years of sobriety. We younger ones were shocked by her behavior. She further shocked us by wearing pants. The women from our vil-lage always had worn dresses, and few women wore pants. It was something we had gotten used to, and when our own mother put on pants we had to alter the way we thought about her. Instead of this quiet woman who always obeyed our father, we saw a woman with a mind of her own. A part of us did not like this change in her, for it made us feel that she was being disloyal to my father. It would take years before I finally saw that my mother had every right to be her own person.

Friends in sixth grade changed too. Some grew taller; some started smoking cigarettes and acting more grown-up. The girls were hanging out with the more popular kids. I gravitated toward the rowdy girls who had drunken parents.

One day, my friend Patty stole eight hundred dollars worth of food stamps from her drunken parents, and she invited me and a couple of other friends on a shopping spree. Buying anything our deprived hearts wanted was a heady experience. Although the store clerk ob-viously disapproved, she did not say anything but only grimaced.

We carried our brown paper bags of goodies to our math class and, laughing and chatting, laid out our fare on one of the long tables. We were unaware that our classmates and the teacher had stopped what they were doing and were staring at us in disbelief. We fully intended to gorge ourselves as we did our math.

Our math teacher had grown up in Fort Yukon and probably thought he had seen all there was to see. He had seen changes in our behavior, but perhaps he had not wanted to believe that it would go that far, for he had kept trying to discipline us gently, as if we were still the innocent and disciplined children we once had been.

A dark shade of red traveled up his neck to his face. He walked to our table and slammed his fist down on it, asking us what in the hell we thought we were doing.

We were astonished. Being unsupervised at home, it never occurred to us that in the outside world there were rules we were expected to obey.

We stared at our teacher with open mouths. He must have seen something defiant in our faces, for he ordered us out of his class. The other students smirked as we held our heads down, packing up our bags of chips, pop, and candy. We wondered what was this man's problem. But in our teenage arrogance, we were only momentarily taken aback as we went into a building across the street and snuck into the bathroom, munching our junk food and trying to make sense of it all.

* * *

That spring after my father's death, a liquor store opened in Fort Yukon. My younger siblings came running home with coin banks shaped like Schlitz beer cans, but by the time I got down to the new store the supplies of this freebie had run out.

That was the last thing the liquor store ever gave out for free. Tax revenue from liquor in time would provide Fort Yukon with a police department, cable television, and village administrators. The liquor itself contributed more graves than one wants to count.

The combination of monthly welfare checks and the local liquor store gave people like my mother carte blanche to drink to their hearts' content.

I was not judgmental about this until years later. At the time I was ecstatic. We were free. There were no rules, practically everyone was drunk, and life was good for us little ones who until recently had been ruled with an iron hand.

When I went to the school in May to collect my grades, one of the more outspoken teachers said to me and my friends, "You've got some kind of nerve! You guys didn't even go to school!" Again we were perplexed at this anger directed our way.

A friend tried to get me to smoke but I refused. Soon after my father died, I had made a bargain with God. If he protected my mother,

In the early 1970s, I did not want my world to change
any more. But I was blossoming into a hideous thing
called womanhood.

I would never drink, smoke, or do drugs. If I broke a promise, I felt
sure that God would take my mother.

The more I rejected friendly offers to drink or smoke, the more
out of place I felt among my friends. I became more and more with-
drawn until I felt like an outcast and could no longer bear the taunts
of my former friends, who felt I could be saved if only I would accept
a drink or a cigarette.

I did not want the world to change any more. I was blossoming
into the hideous thing called womanhood. I couldn't hide my devel-
oping breasts; my periods were messy and made me ill each month.
My mother did not have time to talk to me about this stage of my life
as she had done with my sister Martha. I had heard her telling Martha
that she became a woman when she had her first period. To me being
a woman meant getting married, having children, and doing all the things
I had watched my mother do. I vowed that I would never submit to a
man like my father, nor would I emulate my mother.

✳ ✳ ✳

That summer, my mother sent me to spend a few months in Anchorage with her sister Dorothy, whom I had never met. As I boarded the airplane, I felt sad leaving my family, but my mother assured me that Aunt Dorothy desperately needed my help with the two grandchildren she had adopted. I waved goodbye to my four brothers and little sister as they cried, holding onto my mother's hands.

Arriving in Anchorage, I felt completely disoriented. My aunt was talkative, and as we drove to her house in Mountain View I said nothing as she talked on and on. She explained that she had taken these two little girls, who were two and three, away from her daughter and was determined to raise them herself.

Aunt Dorothy's way of raising children was strict. She gave me a long list of chores, and despite the fact that I had never managed a household, I attempted to do so while she worked all day long. She treated me more as a maid and nanny than a visiting relative.

It was a lonely summer. At times I would mingle with the neighborhood children, who were Hispanic. They were nice children, and we had fun playing games in the street. Old Shirley, who was my aunt's neighbor, constantly lifted her lace curtains to see what I was up to. Most of the time I kept a low profile, for she told my aunt everything she saw that day.

When she told my aunt that I played with the Hispanic children from down the street, I was forbidden to play with those kids, whom my aunt said were "the worst kind."

I grew to detest Old Shirley for her tattling ways. I kept out of range of her snooping eyes and continued playing with my forbidden friends.

When Aunt Dorothy spent time with me, she loved talking. Her stories were always wild and filled with unbelievable adventure. She told me one story about a time when she wore a wraparound skirt and a big truck zoomed past her and the skirt came loose and fell off.

Yet there were times I listened carefully, for her face would become serious as she talked about her ex-husband. He was abusive and a stalker. He had vowed one day to kill her, so she kept a .45 caliber pistol fully loaded at the top of her closet just in case he kept his promise. Her fears filled me, and after hearing about him, I lay awake late into the night.

One day my aunt was invited to a wedding. She said she would be gone until at least midnight. I put the girls to bed and then sat awake imagining all the horrible things that might happen to us in my aunt's absence. One of them was the ex-husband.

I went around the small house and tightly locked all the windows and doors. Then I took the gun down from the closet, pulled back the hammer, and lay back on my aunt's pillow awaiting any sinister intrusion.

I awoke in my bed the next morning. Later, my aunt gave me a big lecture on guns and what damage they could do, saying she would never trust me again. I listened, but the night of my fear was over, so I did not think I would need the gun again.

Besides talking, my aunt also loved to rummage through thrift stores. When she had a little money left over from her single income, she took me to the thrift stores and we would dig around to our hearts' content.

Once we were walking home by a housing project when my aunt suddenly stiffened, taking my hand roughly and telling me not to look. I looked.

Black people sat on the stoops outside the main entrance of identical apartment complexes, taking in the heat of the summer day. Some smiled our way, others just basked in the sunshine. One waved, and I felt an inner tug to respond, but my aunt said, "Don't look at them!", her lips tightening. I sensed fear and obeyed, looking away until we were in the clear.

A safe distance away, she began berating black people. I don't remember exactly what she said, for her list of complaints was long. I just listened, with no way of knowing whether she was telling the truth or not.

That summer in Anchorage enlightened me about the ways of the city. According to my aunt and others that I came in contact with, the whites were okay but people of color were suspect.

When the summer came to an end, my aunt wanted me to stay. She said I needed a good education and the city would give me that. But at thirteen, I wasn't so sure, for I felt she wanted to make me her permanent nanny. I told her I wanted to go home and she grudgingly bought me a ticket home.

＊ ＊ ＊

That fall, my sister Hannah and her husband, Tony, invited us to live with them in Eagle. My mother chartered an airplane up to Eagle, a village almost 300 miles to the south, close to the border between Alaska and Canada. There we lived for three months before my mother decided that living in another village was not good for us. That spring, after our return to Fort Yukon, we felt like strangers in our own village.

My mother struggled with her drinking off and on. Barry and I began skipping school the next school year. My mother did not know how to handle this, so she sent us both up to Chalkyitsik to go to school there. We stayed with Grandpa Mo, who was more than willing to help his daughter.

Barry and I were wild kids. We loved having fun and never gave a second thought to how our wild play might affect others. We did not get along at times, and the fights we would get into were horrible. I choked him, he slugged me, and we were bent on hurting each other. My grandpa had not realized we were so out of control.

When we weren't trying to kill each other, we teased the bachelors of the community by knocking on their doors and running away. We stole Jell-O packages from the school's storage room and ate the powder raw out of the package. We loved to rile the cook, and she told us she knew we were the culprits and that if she caught us we would know her anger. We loved that threat!

One day in class, the kids planned to raid the principal teacher's office, so we planted a lookout. His job was to whistle, but when he spotted the returning teacher, he discovered that he didn't know how to whistle, so we got caught big time.

Another time we had a food fight in the classroom. The teacher was outraged beyond words. But he was a fair man and did not throttle us, as past teachers might have. Instead he made us clean up our mess as he sternly lectured.

One day, the teacher took me into his office. He cleared his throat nervously and told me we needed to discuss a delicate matter. I wondered what could be so delicate.

When he finally got to his point, I was mortified to learn that my not wearing a bra was becoming uncomfortably noticeable. I hadn't noticed that my breasts had grown. I was immature and ignored the changes around me, and myself. After our talk, I became painfully aware of my body, and I wore layers of shirts—and a heavy jacket later on—to hide it.

At home, Grandpa Mo tried to make us into honest people. Many times, he ended up throwing up his hands in frustration and going off to visit his friends.

We stayed out until late at night, but in the early morning my grandfather diligently awoke us for school. Every morning Grandpa Mo would cook us sunnyside-up eggs. We were not used to this kind of cooking, so Barry and I would excuse ourselves and go into the back bedroom, where we would dump the eggs out the window. It never occurred to us to tell Grandpa Mo we didn't like our eggs cooked that way.

One day when we came home from school, Grandpa Mo sat us down for one of his talks.

"You guys hurt my feelings." he said, "Here I am, trying my best to help your mother with you, and you return the favor by insulting my cooking." He had gone to the back of his house to do some yardwork and was surprised to discover a couple weeks' worth of sunnyside-up eggs dumped there.

Barry and I were embarrassed, but still we did not admit that we disliked our eggs cooked that way. Instead we promised him we would not do it again. So, like a couple of dummies, we learned to like our eggs sunnyside-up.

Grandpa Mo gave us the responsibility of feeding his dogs. Barry hated that chore and made sure he was nowhere to be found at feeding time. Barry preferred doing the indoor chores, so I did the outside jobs. The local kids teased us about this. But there were times when Barry and I did jobs together, like going down to the river to haul water on a beautifully moonlit night.

Grandpa Mo carefully instructed me on how to feed his dogs. I would fill the dogs' bowls with two cups of Friskies and a slice of tallow. Remembering what ferocious appetites my father's dogs had, sometimes I fed the dogs two times a day. I did not want them to get too hungry.

Near Thanksgiving, my grandfather's dogs began dying on a daily basis. A woman who lived along the road to the dump said that every day she saw Grandpa Mo go by with a sad hunch to his shoulders, pushing his sled with a dead dog on it.

"What's going on?" she asked, but I had no answer.

One day, we found Grandpa Mo drunk on the steps of his house. We helped him inside, and he told us that his last and favorite dog, named *Na'in*, had died.

"I don't know what I did, but my dogs are all dead," he wept. "My best buddy *Na'in* is dead now."

Our hearts went out to Grandpa in his grief. Never had I seen a man cry so hard over dogs.

I had to acknowledge to myself that I might be guilty for feeding the dogs twice a day. I didn't want them to starve and had figured two feedings were better than one. My grandfather left this world years later, without ever knowing who killed his best buddy.

I never had the courage to tell him while he was alive, for I feared he would not love me anymore. But I did everything I could to make life better for Grandpa Mo. I cleaned, I cooked, I packed water, and I tried to behave myself.

✳ ✳ ✳

One Saturday, Barry and I awoke to find Grandpa Mo in a jovial mood. His friend Henry Williams was visiting, and they were going to spend the day reminiscing.

Barry and I were glad to see Grandpa having fun, especially after losing all his dogs. That afternoon, I found the door to the cellar open. A black tarp was sticking out, and there under it was a barrel of home-brew.

"Oh, darn!" Grandpa said. Wearing a sideways grin, he gently moved me to one side to close the door. "Now you know my secret," he said unapologetically. By then I was frowning.

Grandpa Mo had a nasty habit of drooling when he passed out. That night when he crawled into his mummy bag, he zipped it all the way up to his neck. After the fire in the woodstove died, his spit froze solid along the zipper. Barry and I had to chop him out of his bag with a table knife the next morning.

Just before Christmas, everyone in the village seemed to be sneaking around drinking. My friend said she knew where her father hid his whiskey, so we managed to steal it from the attic one night. We were determined to find out what it was like to be drunk. The whiskey was the most disgusting thing I ever tasted. The stench rose into my nostrils and it burned my throat, but we kept drinking until we were drunk as two thirteen-year-olds could be.

We threw up in my grandfather's bathroom. He wanted to know if we were drunk. We denied it. It must have been blatantly apparent that we were soused, but Grandpa Mo did not press us. We returned to our vomiting.

The next day we were introduced to one of the common side effects of getting drunk: the hangover. Nothing we did made us feel better, and I promised myself that I would never drink again.

The incident with the whiskey bottle would be my last chance to be young and foolhardy for a long time. My grandfather decided we were too much for him to handle, so he sent us back to Fort Yukon. Awaiting there was more responsibility than I had ever known.

CHAPTER THIRTEEN

Back Home

*B*ack in Fort Yukon, my mother was drinking more. For the first time in her life, she could walk away from her responsibilities. Drinking made it possible for her to ignore the needs of her children.

I tried to stay in school, but whenever Mom was not home I found tasks that demanded my attention. The house needed cleaning. Meals needed cooking. Clothes needed washing. The more housework there was to do, the less important school seemed.

By then I had become shy around my peers. Staying home was easier than having to face old friends who had changed beyond recognition. Part of me wanted to act grown-up too, but without the drinking and smoking. So I tried to bypass my teenage years and move directly into my mother's position. I felt that this would insulate me from the changing world outside. I would stay home and play house.

Two teachers who did not want me to quit school sent books down to the house so that I might study at home, but I was a lost cause. As my mother was drawn into alcoholism, I played her role in the family.

I was glad to be the pretend mom. There was Barry, who would always seem older than I was, and at times when I became a recluse, he would act as the go-between for the world and me. Billy, Brady, Benny, and Becky were the younger ones that Barry and I cared for when Mom was not around.

Since our childhood, my mother had done everything for Barry and me. Now it was time for us to do things on our own. When I cooked my first hamburger patty, it shrank to a fraction of its original size. We pondered how to keep it from getting so small as we ate the tiny burgers along with the flaky instant mashed potatoes that I never mixed well enough.

My mother never used a cookbook. Even when making bread she would dig out her big bowl and proceed to add all of the ingredients by memory. When I cooked, I had to recall what I had seen her do. My siblings would try to help.

Once I tried to cook duck soup, and my older brother Johnny, who was visiting that day, taste-tested it. He kept shaking his head as if trying to pinpoint the cause of its funny flavor. Finally he said, "Oh, I know what's going on!"

"You forgot to singe off the feathers," he explained, pulling a couple duck feathers out of his mouth. He could have helped with the cooking, but he and the two other older brothers, Jimmy and David, had their own lives and we hardly ever saw them.

After my father died, the food he had caught and stored the season before slowly ran out, and my mother applied for food stamps. It took us a while to adjust to Mom's decision to use the vouchers, remembering how my father had frowned on the idea.

In the past, Uptown people came down to ask my father for fish and meat. My father was always generous, so even after his death the women from Uptown asked for food. I would get angry and swear a blue streak at them. Could they not see that without my father we no longer had any wild food in our freezer?

We were lucky that my father had a few friends who remembered him. Every Christmas morning, Sampson Peter Jr. from Uptown came down to give us two large king salmon. We looked forward to this feast, for our diet now consisted of what our monthly food stamps could buy at the store. We bought wieners, hamburger, and chicken, as well as staples like sugar, tea, macaroni, rice, butter, Pilot Boy crackers, and grease.

Our meals were not balanced, for we would devour all the crackers with tea in a matter of days. Our bodies were always craving food, and most of the time we ate poorly and gained weight.

* * *

In the years she drank, my mother made it her pattern to drink for two weeks straight every month. For the other two weeks that she was sober, my mother shopped, filling the cupboards and the freezer with food. She would bake loaves of bread and a big pan of biscuits for us. After doing all of this, she got a certain look in her eyes, and we knew her time on the streets was fast approaching. Her two weeks of sobriety usually ended with her putting on her jacket, telling us that she was going to go visiting and would be back shortly. Often two full weeks would pass before she returned.

Sometimes she returned home drunk and fought with us. She accused us of stealing her wine and her food stamps, and would try to bully us as my father once did. She cried about the past, and then threatened that if we didn't shape up she would throw us out of the house. The list of what she said and did was long, and most of the time we learned to listen to her, knowing it was only the drink that made her do those things. But when she brought home her street friends and they tried to use the house for drinking, I would have to fight them all. Then my mother and I would literally have a fist fight. When she managed to hit me, I felt like I hated her.

Once one of her friends had diarrhea all over the place, and I had to clean our house from ceiling to floor to get rid of the smell. I cleaned up her friend and ushered all of her friends out of the house, even though they looked like they needed to be hospitalized, they were so ill from drinking. Those were the times I wished they would all die, including my mother. I rationalized that they were better off dead.

When she sobered up, we loved her as if nothing had happened. But I was fast growing into a hateful teenager. I hated alcohol with a passion. I would rather die than touch the stuff.

✳ ✳ ✳

The 1970s were a time when everyone in Fort Yukon seemed to be drinking. A whole generation of us spent our teenage years with no concept of rules, discipline, or order. Nor did we feel safe at any time of day.

One night, a drunk crept into the house and sat by the couch where I was sleeping. When I woke I escorted him out of the house. From then on, the doors were kept locked.

Often a neighbor would come running wild-eyed to tell us about someone being killed or maimed uptown. We all seemed addicted to bad news. If someone didn't get killed, raped, or stabbed Friday or Saturday night, then on Sunday night people would suffer from withdrawal.

Even my older brothers joined in the fray of violence. One of my older brothers once came from Uptown staggering drunk and decided to bother us. He started a chainsaw and began to chase us with it. We were horrified. Not knowing what kind of drugs he was on, we ran for our lives to the nearby clinic to call the police. The nurse on duty was a crusty old soul who had been there for more years than she cared to count, and when we begged to use her phone she became disgusted with the whole situation.

"You people never learn!" she said, slamming the door in our faces.

We stood on the porch and wondered who else we could turn to for our protection as the cold winter wind touched our faces in the night. We knew then that no one could or would protect us. Even if the police showed up, they were just as burnt out and bitter as the nurse, so we had to hide until our brother sobered up.

Another time this brother got drunk and kicked down the door of our cabin, acting as if he would stab me. My mother, who was also drunk, went down on her knees and begged him not to do it. I stood there hoping he would.

In time I came to hate my older brothers. It riled me to no end that when they were sober they did not seem to remember the terrors they had inflicted on the rest of us.

$$* \; * \; *$$

Christmas always meant hardship for me. One Christmas when my father was still alive, I caught my younger siblings eating the scraps that I had scraped into a pan as I cleaned the mounds of pots, pans, and dishes. I cried as I watched them eat the scraps, but there was nothing I could do—they were hungry and there was nothing else to eat.

Barry and I tried to make Christmas festive for the younger ones. We never had money for presents, but our sister Linda, the only sister still living in town, made sure we each had a gift and some candy. Despite the fact that she supported her family of four, she always tried to help us no matter how it strained her budget.

Only once did Barry and I plan a month ahead and order a few gifts for the kids from the Sears, Roebuck catalog. We sat on pins and needles, right up until midnight on Christmas Eve. The postmaster was a young man who understood our plight. He kept the post office open late for those who were still waiting for our packages to arrive. I thought it akin to a miracle when our box arrived that night.

It got to the point that the less we had in the way of a family, the more we tried to fill the void with material goods. Christmas became an obsession. Barry and I dreamed of having a good Christmas, which

Things hadn't changed much when I returned to Fort Yukon in 1980.
I decided I wanted to learn trapping and living off the land.

meant a sober mother and a time of togetherness like our family once
had. When things did not work out that way, we would just call it a bad
Christmas.

✳ ✳ ✳

When I was sixteen, I worked for a program called Homehelpers.
My job was to clean the house of an old woman named Blanche Strom.

Blanche was confined to a wheelchair. She reminded me of an
owl with those watchful eyes that neither smiled nor acknowledged
you in any way. She wanted her house sparkling clean, and she missed
nothing. More than once she took the mop out of my hands and showed
me how to mop the floor properly.

"You kids today just want everything easy," she barked at me as
she briskly mopped the floor. She did not seem to need any help as
she wheeled herself about, showing me how she wanted her dishes
washed and her floors cleaned. It seemed that the only thing she
couldn't do was empty her chamber pot outside.

One day, Blanche sat eyeing me as I mopped her floor. Sweat dripped down my nose, and my face was red with exertion. I was trying to get the job done quickly so I could escape her scrutiny.

"How come you guys never use your father's land?" she asked.

I did not know how to respond. I had not thought about my father's trapline since Itchoo had tried to save her tree years before.

The old woman persisted.

"Don't you know that if you don't use that land, it will be taken over by others?" she demanded.

I nodded, but I did not care.

"Your grandmother Martha Wallis used that land too. You guys should use it instead of wasting it. Already I hear that a young man is taking over your land. You need to use that land before it's too late."

I finished mopping and nodded my head as if I intended to take her advice. In reality I just wanted to go home.

A day later Blanche died. She had seemed perfectly lively the day before. I could not bring myself to collect the pay owed to me, for in some ways she had given me the first inkling of respect that I had had in years.

Later I questioned Jimmy about the land. Jimmy, who was four years older and once had been my tormentor, was now the quiet brother. He didn't say much, but what he did say always made complete sense.

"There's nothing there," Jimmy said. "It's all burnt out. Me and Alex tried to trap there, but there's nothing to trap so we just left."

"Take me up there," I told my brother.

At first he thought I was joking. When he realized that I was serious, he told me to pack. He would take me to my family's trapline.

Being on my own as a teenager allowed me to recklessly do whatever popped into my mind. Jimmy was used to my adventurous spirit, and he knew once I decided on something it would be a waste of time trying to change my mind.

I wanted to learn to trap and to live off the land. The younger kids were bigger now, and we all had learned to become latchkey kids, independent in our own way. Billy and Brady had begun the early stages of dropping out of school. As my mother had tried to keep Barry and me in school to no avail, I tried to do so with them but I never bothered them too much about school because they hauled firewood and snared rabbits when they weren't in school. Without them, we would not have had firewood or rabbit meat. The younger children, Benny and Becky, were able to care for themselves too.

Blanche had set in my mind a romantic notion about Itchoo's land. I was intrigued that it belonged to us, for we had nothing. Fort Yukon had become quite predictable. I wanted to know what was out there. My mother had always spoken fondly of the land she and my father had lived on in the first years of their marriage. They had many adventures up there, and the fur had been plentiful. I wanted to be a trapper like my father and grandmother.

Many times I had watched my father pack for a trip into the woods. Trying to remember what he had taken, I gathered up all the necessary supplies: Swede saw, ax, knife, file, lots of matches, first-aid kit, camping candles, flashlight, a wooden grub-box filled with kitchen implements, and a couple cardboard boxes filled with store-bought food, plus my clothes and books.

I asked my younger siblings if they wanted to join me on this adventure, and only Billy, who was two years younger, volunteered. Billy was a reluctant participant in all of my endeavors only because he was tender-hearted toward those who come up with nutty ideas. He must have felt sorry for his goofy older sister who always tried crazy things. He said he knew how to trap. But he wanted to join up with me later, for he said he would have to gather his own supplies and find some dogs. So I felt I was set for the winter.

Together, Jimmy and I piled all the supplies on the narrow toboggan and strapped them down. We were ready to head out into the woods.

YUKON FLATS

Neegoo Gwandah

Traditional hunting lands

Father's Fish Wheel

PORCUPINE

Yukon River

Fort Yuk

NeegooGwandah

Sucker River

Winter Trail

YUKON FLATS

Fathers Fish Wheel

CHAPTER FOURTEEN

Neegoogwandah

*T*he November day was sunny and warm as I stood on the back of the narrow sled and fought off the willows and thorns that slapped at my face. The land was void of trees except for these hulking skeletons that stood ominously against the sky. I felt as if I had traveled to another planet.

Jimmy was taking me to Spider Island, which was in the middle of a large lake. He said that when he and our brother-in-law had camped there once, their tent had been swamped with big, black spiders.

With his little Elan Skidoo, Jimmy broke trail along the frozen lake. I kept falling off the toboggan, a long, narrow sled framed with hickory, and covered with untanned moosehide. When I was younger I was afraid of riding behind a sled. Often when we were allowed to use my father's dogs, they sped seemingly without concern for the riders on the sled. When we fell off, it hurt, so I developed a phobia about sleds. Instead of trying to learn the fine art of balancing on a quick-moving sled, I became one of those riders who are always toppling off. My siblings had given up on me in this matter, and on that day as I kept falling off the toboggan, Jimmy tried to have patience with me.

Jimmy dropped the supplies and me off at Spider Island. Then he turned the snowmobile around to go back to Fort Yukon to pick up another load.

Before he left, Jimmy said, "When I get back, the tent should be up and there should be a pot of hot tea on the stove."

On Jimmy's next trip, Billy tagged along to see what "our" trapline looked like before he moved up. When they arrived, I was trying to figure out how to put up the eight-by-eight canvas tent.

Jimmy sighed in exasperation. In a matter of minutes he chopped down long spruce poles and propped the tent up. Billy helped him. Then they threw a bunch of spruce boughs and pieces of wood on the ground, doused them with gas, and lit a fire. Jimmy took the blackened teapot from one of my boxes, swooped snow into it, and set it on the fire so that the snow would melt. Digging around in my grub-box, he found my container of loose tea. He threw a handful of it into the teapot, which by then was full of hot, bubbling water.

"Geez, I thought there would be a pot of tea by the time I returned," he said. "You just can't stand around when you're out here. You have to move around and get things done."

He instructed me to find spruce boughs for my bedding and suggested I start gathering loose wood from under the snow now, for darkness was approaching.

When Jimmy and Billy had finished their tea, they became restless. I tried to keep them around, but they were impatient to go home. When I could hold them no longer, I made Billy promise he would return. He promised.

Jimmy looked at me for a second and asked if I would be all right. I nodded my head confidently. I knew they were expecting me to chicken out. My years of juvenile delinquency had left me proud and outwardly tough. I could not let them know I was petrified.

* * *

Growing up, I thought I had known fear the many times I walked home from school in the dark or had to feed the sled dogs alone. But the fear that settled upon me after my brothers headed back to Fort Yukon left me cold and empty.

I was not going to admit defeat. I set upon the task of getting more wood and making my tent cozy. As night approached, I lit candles. I kept lighting candles until about three in the morning, when I found I had used up what I had thought would be my candle supply for the whole winter.

The next day, I moved about wearily, cutting and chopping wood. That year we had a lot of snow. All of the burnt, fallen trees had to be dug out from under three feet of snow, and then I would saw them into blocks. I had brought along a plastic sled, which I used all that day to haul wood across the lake to my camp. By nightfall I was exhausted and barely had the strength to melt water to cook my supper.

I looked into my grub-box filled with Spam, beans, flour, macaroni, rice, sugar, tea, and crackers—just what I had seen my father pack for a winter on the trapline. The problem was that my father was a hunter and could easily supplement the dry goods with moose meat and rabbits. My only skill was snaring rabbits, and I was afraid to set snares, for if I found a live rabbit in one of my snares I would have to kill it by holding its neck and squeezing its heart, as my mother had taught me to do. I was in the rabbits' territory now and did not feel that I wanted to eat them just yet, so I lived on my supplies.

One spring I took my mother onto the land, and she taught me how to trap muskrat. Here, I am setting the trap.

On my second night, I awoke to a freezing tent. It was the middle of the night, and I was shivering in my sleeping bag. The little aluminum stove gave out a lot of heat but could not hold much wood. So each time the fire died out while I slept I would get up and restart it. The cold air outside easily penetrated the tent and woke me.

Groggily, I tore pieces from one of the boxes that lined my tiny tent, and started another fire. The stove's top had come loose so I placed it on the floor.

Moments later, I turned back and laid my hand right on top of the hot stove lid.

I yelped in pain. I could almost hear the sizzling of my skin. I jumped up and stepped on the stove lid with my bare foot. Again I heard skin burning.

That night I suffered as my skin blistered white and puffy. I downed some aspirin, and in time sleep found me.

For a couple days, I limped around trying to stay warm. I had brought a Swede saw and spent my days cutting firewood until I thought I'd go crazy. But as the days passed, I began to enjoy my time at the saw.

It was hard to hold the log still as I sawed, so I decided to construct a sawhorse. I didn't have nails so I used the picture-hanging wire that we use for rabbit snares to brace the sawhorse together. It held beautifully for that whole winter.

In late morning, I would watch what daylight there was come up over the eastern horizon. While I was still cutting wood in the late afternoon, the sky toward Fort Yukon would turn pink, purple, and blue.

The only evidence I had that I was near Fort Yukon was the sound of an airplane overhead when the daily flights came in from Fairbanks. The rest of the time was silent with no interruption—not even the cry of a raven, nothing.

I looked at my cozy tent with wood piled all around it, and inside everything was neatly in its place. My many little trails were well established. The only thing that remained to do was to set traps. I decided to go down to Fort Yukon and get my trapping partner. He just needs a little encouragement from me, I thought, so I packed my packsack and started down a trail. My foot had healed a little but was still tender as I gingerly limped along.

The way back to Fort Yukon was easy. But there were a couple of snowmachine trails made from trappers who traveled farther from Fort Yukon, and those trails confused me.

From my camp, I knew that I had to travel over two lakes, a couple small portages, and down a bank onto a long and winding slough, called Eight Mile Slough, and Nina Slough, named after my Aunt Nina, to the Sucker River. The river was narrow and often dried up in the summer. From there a road had been opened up years before by one of Fort Yukon's pioneers by the name of Ivar Petersen, for whom the road was named. The walk was about six miles.

Just a couple miles along Ivar's Road I had a choice to keep following the long, winding trail or to turn off to another winding way. The second trail was made by narrow snowmachines along deep, rich brown willows that led to a curved lake named after my grandfather David Wallis's sister, Laura. She had always trapped the lake for muskrats, and people in her time knew that lake was hers to trap.

After getting off Laura Lake, then there was Ivar's Road again, and at some point as I kept walking I spotted the first distant electrical lights that led to one of the FAA's outposts.

The whole time that I walked, I saw no one. The air was about twenty below, and when I had started out the sun was bright and shining, but now night was here and it seemed colder. My ears strained for suspicious sounds, possibly made by a pack of hungry wolves or a mean wolverine. It took years upon the land outside Fort Yukon before I knew that one would be lucky to spot a fox.

To keep myself from getting too scared, I thought about my brother Billy. What was delaying him? Was he sick? What was he up to?

When I arrived at the Fort Yukon airstrip, I was exhausted. I just wanted to lie down on the ground and give up this whole project of saving the family trapping lands.

It would not do to fall asleep and freeze at the end of this lonely airstrip, so with great effort I pulled myself off the ground. My last two miles to my mother's cabin were slow and laborious. Finally, I saw a welcoming light beaming from within the cabin. The boys were still up. I hoped someone had made a tasty stew, for the eight-hour walk had left me famished.

Coming onto the porch, I looked through the window. Inside I could see all my brothers watching television. Billy sat atop a chair and leaned intently toward the screen.

When I burst through the door, they were surprised.

"Hey, you came back," one of them said.

I was angry. Billy quickly explained that he had been planning to come up the next day. I should have known Billy's promises were suspect. He had a habit of telling me whatever I wanted to hear. In reality, he probably never intended to live in a tent that winter.

I allowed myself to be pacified by Billy's explanations because I had no other option. My brothers had not asked to be brought into my project. I was always trying to chart new territory or do something new. In my zeal to prove that something was possible, I always asked my brothers for help. Most of the time they were reluctant because they just wanted to stay in town and watch television.

In the spring of 1976, my mother had burst into our cabin carrying a thirteen-inch black-and-white television. It was never turned off unless the television station went off the air. Many of the shows were reruns, but no matter how many times they showed *Tora, Tora, Tora* or the same old basketball games, we were captivated. It has taken our family more than twenty years to become discriminating about TV shows. My brothers in particular loved television and became addicted to it, especially Billy.

I shouldn't have been too surprised that Billy did not want to leave town and miss his favorite shows. The idea of living in the woods for a few months was unthinkable to him, but he did not let me know that. He kept me believing that he would love to join me in my quest to become a full-fledged trapper. But instead of coming right out and telling me that he did not want to trap, he played along with me right up until I would get the hint. In our family we had a way of saying yes when we wanted to say no and vice versa. We didn't know how to be blunt.

＊ ＊ ＊

After spending almost a week at home, resting and healing my foot, I was ready to go back to Neegoogwandah. Except for my brother Jimmy, we younger ones didn't own a snowmobile. I was prepared to walk back to the camp but Billy was not. He borrowed three big hulking dogs from his trapper friend. My father had once owned dog sleds, but after his death, they disappeared. Now all we had was a Rider sled, the kind we used to slide downhill. It could hold two of us, but when I went outside the house, ready to go, and saw those three big dogs harnessed to that little sled, I told my brother there was no way I was getting on.

Billy looked at the three Siberian huskies that stood harnessed to the tiny sled, waiting patiently. He seemed completely unaware of how ridiculous the huge dogs and the tiny sled looked together.

"It's the only sled I own," he said in a take-it-or-leave-it voice.

I decided to trust my brother despite many past mishaps with him. As we loaded the small sled, I thought that maybe we could get by without being seen by our neighbors.

Comforted by this thought, I sat down on the little sled. Billy knelt down on the back.

"Mush!" he called out to the dogs.

They took off immediately. They looked so big and clumsy that I was not prepared for their speed. I did not know if they understood my brother's commands, but off they went along the trail.

Just as we hit the first turn, the sled tipped and Billy fell off.

"Don't worry!" he called as I hung on. "I'll catch up!"

I tried to turn and saw my brother kneeling on the ground where he had fallen off. We were approaching a cabin and a pack of dogs there barked ferociously. The three dogs and the sled headed straight toward the pack. A few men outside the cabin watched, amused, as I held onto the sled and we drew closer.

Just before we reached the pack, I jumped off the sled. In seconds our three dogs were in a vicious fight with the others.

The owner of the dogs came out of his cabin and started beating the whole lot of them, eventually bringing them under control. By then Billy had caught up to us and retrieved his team.

At first I did not want to get back onto that sled, but Billy had a way of sweet-talking me. He promised there would be no more mishaps. I felt a little foolish sitting on the sled, but Billy assured me that it made traveling light for him and the dogs. The ride up to Neegoogwandah was uneventful after that.

* * *

That afternoon Billy regaled me with tales of his many adventures. I got caught up in my brother's stories despite the fact that he had lived the same sheltered life I had.

The next day, we took my father's old traps and set out to prove ourselves chips off the old block. I had spent the past week rereading one of my father's trapping books, written by a trapper from the Lower 48. Since we had no one to teach us, I had to rely on the book and my brother's knowledge.

The land was nothing but burnt downfalls and tall dead spruce trees that stood out eerily against the November sky. We made our way over huge trunks that stuck out black against the snow.

Soon we found tracks that Billy said had been made by a marten. Later my mother would tell me that they were actually ptarmigan tracks.

"Martens like burnt country," Billy explained, showing me how to set traps in crevices under the tree trunks.

I listened carefully, enraptured by my younger brother's know-how. I believed that because he spent a lot of time with his pals in Fort Yukon, he had gathered more information than I had. After all, he knew how to set a trap.

After we had set our traps, Billy said there was nothing else to do but go back to the camp and wait, but he soon became restless. A couple of hours later he said he had to go back to Fort Yukon for more supplies. I knew he was lying, but I could not hold him back.

He hitched his dogs up to the sled and waved at me.

"I'll be back!" he said.

The dogs immediately took off across the frozen lake into a pile of deadfalls. Billy cussed and stormed at them until they got back on track again.

Again he waved at me, and I sighed, waving back. I had to accept that Billy was not an outdoorsman. I turned back to my tent, knowing that if I wanted to do anything out here, I would have to face the wilderness on my own.

CHAPTER FIFTEEN
Learning New Skills

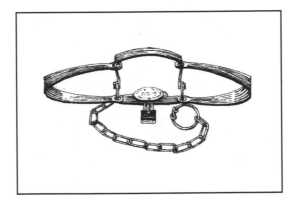

*T*wo days later, I found a foot in one of my traps. I was horrified, imagining how desperate to escape an animal would have to be to gnaw off its own foot. My stomach was in knots as I searched the woods, trying to find the animal, wishing I could undo the damage I had done.

But the animal was gone. Holding its foot, I felt less like a trapper than ever as I trudged back to my tent. This was not what I had imagined. Had my father had to deal with this? Was it worth it to hurt another living being for my own profit? Lord, I knew then that I was not a credit to the proud trappers who had spent their lives out in these woods.

I had embarked on a quest not realizing that there would be consequences. If I was not prepared to deal with the harshness of this lifestyle, maybe I needed to bail out.

I sat in my tent that evening, trying to figure out what kind of animal this little inch-and-a-half foot belonged to, but my knowledge was severely limited. I could hardly sleep for imagining some poor animal hobbling painfully around on one foot. I had nightmares, and I thought that I heard an agonized screech in the night.

My curiosity continued to eat at me the next day, so I embarked on another journey down to Fort Yukon. Although my second walk to town was still long, it seemed easier. Recognizing a ridge, I knew how long it would take, so I paced myself and found countless ways to keep my attitude positive for the miles ahead. When I arrived at home, the boys were again surprised to see me.

I asked them what animal the foot belonged to and, looking at it without much interest, they agreed it belonged to a mouse. I had my doubts. I knew a mouse was much smaller than that.

I was surprised when my mother came out of the back room. In my absence she had sobered up, and she was upset that I was living up at Neegoogwandah. I interrupted her angry tirade to ask her about the foot. She took one look at it and said it was a marten's foot. Then I told her my story, but she still disapproved of what I was doing. In spite of the fact that my mother had grown up self-sufficient and independent in spirit, in spite of the fact that she had lived out on Neegoogwandah by herself with her children at times while my father trapped farther up the country or was drunk in Fort Yukon, she believed that what I was doing was not good for me.

"No woman has ever lived in the woods by herself," she said.

"But you and Itchoo lived out there," I reminded her.

She responded by saying that they had been trained and had grown up in isolation. It would be difficult for me because I had lived a sheltered life.

My mother's warnings came too late. I already had been exposed to life in the woods, and I was enjoying its challenges. Mom had learned long ago that it was not worth her time to argue. I had had my own way for too long and no longer acknowledged anyone's authority.

Despite my squeamishness about trapping animals, I found myself drawn to the strange beauty of Neegoogwandah. The land was so quiet and devoid of obvious signs of life. A whispering silence hovered over the omnipresent stillness of this land that had been ravaged and was slowly being healed by time. I wondered what mysteries it held for me to discover.

I had brought a lot of food when I first went up, and knew that it had to last the whole winter until I could trap muskrats. I lived on Pilot Boy crackers and Spam. I was young and my hunger to continue what I had started outweighed my worries about food. I knew that if I ran out of grub, I was within walking distance of the store.

I didn't stay at home for too long, for Fort Yukon now seemed dreary to me. I longed to see the long stretches of lakes and winding sloughs and my trapping camp.

✳ ✳ ✳

January and February passed in temperatures dipping to fifty below. Even so, I would leave my tent flap open as I lay on my bedding of spruce boughs covered with a sleeping bag. Dry wood blazed inside my little stove as I sipped hot tea and watched the cold winter sky turn all sorts of hues toward Fort Yukon while the sun went down.

I had given up on trapping. Although there was no reason for being on this land anymore, I could not drag myself away. My brothers borrowed snowmachines and came to see what I was doing. They spent nights in my tent and days scouting the land for tracks. Then they would go home before dark.

That spring, the boys said that Mom was drinking too much. I went down to Fort Yukon and found her on one of her binges. I told her she had to leave with me the next day. She balked, afraid that she would go through bad withdrawal symptoms. So I went to the liquor store and bought her a small bottle of whiskey, and then she followed me.

When we reached the first lake, which my mother said was called Frog Lake because of all the tiny frogs that used to live there, our toboggan tipped over and my mother fell face-first into the snow.

Brady was driving the snowmachine, and he got angry that I couldn't seem to keep the toboggan balanced. Where Jimmy had been mildly upset with my poor efforts, Brady cursed at me. I defended myself.

While my brother and I argued, my mom crawled out of the snowdrifts. Her face covered with snow, she looked around. Her red eyes surveyed the land, roving over the tall, blackened trees against the sky and the big black downfalls that stuck out of the snow.

Tears slid down my mother's parched face, yellow from weeks of drinking.

"This land used to be like the Garden of Eden," she said. "We could walk miles without tripping over twigs. It was almost as if someone kept the land clean."

My brother and I looked around, unable to imagine this landscape looking anything other but desolate.

We helped Mom out of the snow and continued on to Spider Island.

* * *

It was hard for Mom to sober up. I nursed her with tea with whiskey, and she spent time retching on the snow. I was a fanatic for cleanliness and made her empty out in one specific area. I wanted to keep this place as pristine as possible.

After a couple of days, I talked my mother into going onto the lake to teach me how to set traps for the muskrats that lived along the lakes under moss tunnels, and under the ice inside a well-constructed moss house. She did not feel up to it, but I was persistent. I had spent the whole winter without instructions and did not want to spend a minute more in ignorance. I wanted knowledge!

Mom barely made it out onto the lake. The cold March wind howled across the flat land, and the snowdrifts were hard, whipped up like white frosting. We searched for a black clump of moss sticking out of the snow on the frozen surface of the lake. When we found one, Mom knelt down and showed me how to uncover the muskrat house.

"The muskrat will always build his house facing the sun," Mom explained, as she used a small ax to chop an opening on the side of the house.

As she dug out the moss, it filled the air with its musty scent. She showed me the muskrat's bedding, then opened a number-one steel trap and placed it expertly down in the hole.

The trap snapped back and caught my mother's unsuspecting fingers. Her face went ashen, and it was minutes before she could open the trap carefully and place it in the muskrat house.

"Be careful with these things," she added. "They will spring back at the slightest touch."

She replaced the moss that she had carved off the opening and covered it with snow, ladling water over it.

"Make sure you always close the hole nice and solid, or it will freeze the muskrat out and the hole will be useless."

With that we went searching for more muskrat houses.

We set thirteen traps that day. Mom told me that when I was out in the woods, I was not to waste one minute sitting around waiting for something to be caught in my traps.

"You have to move around," she said. "No one is going to cut and split your wood. No one is going to snare rabbits for you."

She continued on and on with her long list of things that no one but I could do to help me survive in the woods.

Mom had always done everything for my siblings and me. She never allowed us to tie our own shoes or to zip our own jackets. She was right there to do it all for us, and we never thought to question her or demand our right to be independent. It was almost as if she tried to abate her own guilt at losing Grafton by doing everything for us.

After my father died, she left us by ourselves so often that we had to learn how to survive on our own. Without any instruction, we clumsily found ways to get by. Once when Mom had spent weeks uptown drinking, we were desperate for food and pried the last king salmon out of the bottom of the freezer. We were so hungry that we could hardly wait for the meat to cook, so we ate it half-raw.

Now, for the first time, my mother was teaching one of us her skills. I felt a new sense of my mother as a person, no longer in my father's dominating shadow.

I was her avid student. Each morning and afternoon, we checked our traps. The first time we opened one of the holes to see if we had caught anything, I was appalled to find water bugs of all sizes and shapes filling the hole. I had always disliked bugs because my brothers used to chase us around the yard with bugs in their hands. Since those times bugs had given me the shivers. Now I made retching sounds as I saw that they shared the same space with my favorite food, the muskrat.

"Never talk about your food the wrong way," Mom corrected me. "These bugs are the muskrat's friends."

She gently moved them aside.

"They keep the water hole open." she explained.

I grew up enjoying many meals of muskrat, but once I had trapped them I could never eat them with the same zeal. It's one thing to eat food that is provided to you directly from the stove to the table, but when you see the way an animal becomes food, it is a different story. I never had given thought to the whole food-chain scenario, and having witnessed it, I was in awe of the little animals that lived on the land. It was years before I could relish eating muskrat and beaver meat again.

Mom grew exasperated with me because I would not eat the muskrats we caught. But muskrats are a delicacy, and she did not mind too much that I was not eating my fair share.

My mother and I spent the rest of that spring enjoying the simple life of living in a tent. Each afternoon after we had completed the day's chores, we would open the flap of our tent and lay upon our spruce bough bedding, staring placidly at the sky toward Fort Yukon.

I grew accustomed to the silence that came over the land. Now and then ravens could be heard, but usually they were too busy scavenging the dump in town where trash was plentiful.

In the evening while our supper cooked on the stove, we enjoyed the wonderful colors that enlivened the southwest horizon as the blue sky darkened by the hour.

Finally it was time to move back to Fort Yukon. Living on this land was only good in the winter, when snow could be melted and boiled for cooking. In the summer it was too hard to get clean water.

The winter had been adventurous. People from Fort Yukon had come the distance to visit us during the winter; we provided them with an excuse to go out into the woods again. My brothers were exposed to outdoor life, too. I learned to trap, and my mother began her long journey back to sobriety. It had been a good winter.

CHAPTER SIXTEEN

*T*hat summer, my mother got herself invited to a fish camp, where she helped cut and dry the salmon. At the end of the season her hosts dropped her off at home with a truckload of fish.

When fall came, Jimmy, Billy, Brady, and Benny went up to Neegoogwandah and built a small cabin there. I followed in the spring with rugs, curtains, beds, and other furnishings. Soon we had a cozy cabin.

Mom came back up to stay with me that spring. We now had a communal home where my brothers and their friends could come to visit and hunt.

My mother and I stayed at the cabin, enjoying the company of the many visitors who left their homes to come see what we were up to. One night we had thirteen people in our twelve-by-twelve-foot cabin at Neegoogwandah. We never felt as if we did not have enough space. We were quite content.

* * *

When my brothers impulsively shot a moose out of season my mother realized they needed supervision. They had always done crazy things, and my mom and I had stood back scowling at them, but they always convinced us that what they were doing was okay.

"Never kill a moose out of season!" my mother hollered at them. Recently two Fish and Game wardens had landed their plane outside our Neegoogwandah cabin. They visited for a while, and my mother said they were curious about this new cabin. We would get in serious trouble if they discovered what my brothers had done.

The boys seemed surprised that my mother was unhappy with them. She made us bring the meat to the cabin. I was so nervous I spent the better half of the day and night covering the tracks. Regardless of my efforts, the next day a pilot from town told us that he could see as plain as day that a moose had been killed.

I fretted until it snowed; only then I could breathe easier. The fresh snow covered what I was unable to hide.

Still, it felt good to have fresh meat. I would be a hypocrite if I said that I didn't enjoy the tasty moose meat that year.

* * *

After the moose incident, my mother devoted all her sober moments to teaching us how to hunt, fish, and survive. She had a patience about her that invited us to learn. Many times she would fall back into her old habit of trying to do things for us, but then she would stop and hand us back the knife to try cutting the fish or meat ourselves. Or, she would show us once how to set a trap and let us try it the next time.

Finally we could feel our connection to the land and see our mother in a new light. For me and my siblings a new way of thinking was becoming possible. I had been an angry teenager trapped in an alcoholic village, stuck in the squalor of HUD housing and orange pee stains on the snow, left by local drunks staggering along our paths. Now, being out in the fresh, clean world of nature, I was enlightened by a different way of living.

Still, my mother had a mind of her own. As much as we wanted to hold her hostage at Neegoogwandah to make her stay sober, her drinking pulled her uptown. We would not see her for weeks at a time. Stories circulated about how she helped her friends steal food from their families to support their bad habits. Sometimes she would try to cross the boundaries we had long ago set for her by attempting to take our food uptown to sell. I kept watch.

Each month, we received a whole host of welfare checks, and in her worst moments Mom would try to get them. If she got hold of the welfare money or food stamps, she would pay bills but then spend the rest of the money on alcohol. So I made sure she did not get her hands on them. My mother would cuss and curse, but I would not let her have the checks or else we would not have food.

I could not have done it on my own. Others in the village knew our situation and in their own way helped us survive. The postmaster, for instance, would not place the checks in our mailbox until I came.

As much fun as we had with our mother during her sober days, we learned to hate her drinking and all that it entailed. Especially me. I became depressed by all the struggles with her and other drunken relatives. It seemed that everyone around me built their lives around the liquor store. The years of being around drunks got me so down that once I contemplated suicide. I held a gun to my head, thinking it would be better just to end it all. Then, in a moment of hesitation, I thought of my younger sister, Becky, and my four younger brothers, Barry, Billy, Brady, and Benny. A suicide was the last thing they needed. There was too much shame as it was. So I put the gun down.

* * *

Few people in town cared what happened to kids like us. I remember one woman, Diane, whom I had grown up admiring. She could do no wrong in my eyes, and when I was little I would follow her around like a little lamb. When I called her name, she would squint to see who was calling her, for she needed glasses. Then when she recognized me, she'd burst into a deep, dimpled smile. Diane was the older sister I wanted. My own sisters had moved on and my only role models were the women in the village who drank. In the dark tunnel of my life, Diane was a bright light.

She came to our house bringing me a jar of Stridex skin cleanser and some clothes. She managed to explain that she wanted me to start taking care of myself. At first I was insulted. I could not see that I was allowing myself to become run down. Nor could I accept offers of love or encouragement from anyone. I had been on my own for a while and no one could tell me what to do.

But I could see that Diane was concerned about me, and I still admired her. She was one of the few younger women in Fort Yukon who refrained from drinking, and she was working to earn a teaching degree. She had my respect in a time when I gave it to few people.

When I look back, I realize that no one else could have helped me. Everyone else was so busy drinking that they wouldn't have thought to take aside a depressed young woman and tell her that she was worth better treatment.

It took awhile to build up my self-esteem, but with subtle encouragement from Diane, I found myself jogging, drinking more water, and coming out of my depression.

* * *

At some point, two of my younger brothers started to drink, and soon they joined those who celebrated the long holiday. I was losing ground with my siblings, and I grew bitter.

When I turned eighteen, I succumbed and started to drink too. One of my older siblings was amused to watch me staggering about, and my youngest sibling had to wake me up as I snored into my own vomit.

Not only was I depressing to others, but I found that as a drunk I was more depressed than ever. My brother Jimmy would sit for long hours in the night and listen to my sad stories as I wept inconsolably.

"Geez, Velma, you're not too fun to drink with!" he said to me, and more tears came as I competed with the sad country music we played as we sipped whiskey.

I had so much pent-up emotion that had never been expressed, and when I drank all that emotion came out in violent bursts. I was uncontrollable. I wept for my dead father, for my drunken mother, for the past, for the future. When I could not ease the ache, I sought more liquor to wipe it all from my mind.

Later, a cousin brought in a bag of dope. I felt that I was losing control over all aspects of my life. After I smoked dope, I found myself eating strange foods, like tomatoes sprinkled with tons of sugar, and hanging around people I would not have considered talking to when I was sober.

Then one day I caught a glimpse of how I might end up if I didn't gain some control over my behavior. I was walking slowly down a road, trying to rid myself of a miserable hangover, when I saw a girl my age stumbling blindly out of a man's house, the zipper of her pants wide open. I knew then that if I didn't quit drinking, I would soon be in her shoes.

With much struggle and resolve, I kept away from those who had inducted me into the drinking scene. That was one thing I had noticed—that they seemed to enjoy adding new people to their drinking circles.

In time, people saw me as my strange old self again. I had to accept the fact that I was not willing to pay the high price of being part of the "in" crowd.

Living in Fort Yukon and not drinking or doing drugs meant deciding to be alone. Barry, my sister Becky, and I clung to one another. Barry and Becky had never drunk.

We walked around the village together, visiting people who we knew would be sober. We developed hobbies, such as digging in the

The Neegoogwandah cabin near our family's trapline.

riverbanks where the old village used to be, searching for old bottles and coins. We walked the woods outside town and scavenged the old dump site for antique cans and bottles.

Barry spent his free time painting; I took up beadwork. Becky baby-sat for two women who were attending the local affiliate of the University of Alaska Fairbanks. We grew used to our brothers drinking, and in time that became part of the life we lived in Fort Yukon.

Barry supported me during the times when I became a depressed recluse. People from the village gossiped about my weirdness. Even the old women held their heads and talked in Gwich'in about the *Na'in*—the outsider—and I knew they were referring to me. I held my head low in shame. But Barry would take me aside and tell me that my eccentricity was part of my natural charisma.

"Think about it!" he would say. "No one else in this town is like you. You are unique! Anytime people talk about a person as people talk about you, that makes you different. People hate what's different. They hate what's different because you are not like them. You are in a class of your own, and when they talk, they talk to comfort themselves in their sameness."

After Barry gave me one of those talks, I was on cloud nine for weeks. I felt that I could conquer the world. My self-esteem was so low, but he was so confident in everything he did.

* * *

Mom's drinking began to take a toll on her health, and she struggled to stay sober for longer periods of time. We rallied for her, and when she fell off the wagon we were devastated each time. But then she would try again. We repeated the process over and over.

Sometimes we became impatient for her to quit drinking and we would carry her bodily out of town to fish camp or to our trapline, where she could sober up. She was good for those many weeks, but then she would go back to town and drink again.

The harder my mother worked to control her drinking, the more sober time she had to spend teaching us. Once she took my younger brothers hunting, and they took aim at a moose that was wading through the water. Although she told them not to shoot it until it left the water, one of my brothers shot the moose anyway. They found it quite a challenge to cut apart the moose in the water and to get it into their boat, and they learned their lesson well.

My mother and brothers would go up to Neegoogwandah to trap muskrat and beavers. When the trapping season was over, Mom would return to town to drink again, and this time my brothers came back to drink too.

* * *

Now that the boys were drinking, my sister Becky and I decided to move out of my mother's house. It was too heart-rending to see our brothers stagger around. When I tried to talk sense to them, they became angry and said it was their life.

My Aunt Nina long since had moved to Fairbanks to be near her son Larry, and Becky and I asked her to let us live in her two-room log cabin by the river. She gave us her permission.

Becky and I took our sled out into the woods, cut our own firewood, and hauled it back to the cabin all winter long. Seeing us do this, the city manager assumed we were poor and took pity on us. He offered me my first job, as a police dispatcher.

My first night on the job was something to remember. The city manager told me to answer the phone and to write down everything in the log book. That night women kept phoning and asking for one of the officers. They would tell me it was an emergency, but they wouldn't tell me what their plight was. I was new to this and tried to be of some help.

When I tried to get the officer on the police radio, he responded rudely and was not interested in helping these poor women. He told me not to call again. I was beside myself with worry. What kind of cop was this? If these women couldn't call the police, who could they call?

Another woman kept calling that night, saying that her husband was fighting with her. Try as I might, I could not get any of the three officers to come to aid any of the callers. My stomach churned with worry all night long.

Later, I was to learn more about these police officers. The one who had been rude was a ladies' man. That night he had been trying to behave himself, for he lived with a local woman who was jealous. People said he sold drugs, too, and half of the people who called for him were his regular customers.

I worked with the police department for a while, until they hired a man from Los Angeles. He made it clear right away that he did not like minorities. He didn't like dogs either, so he spent the better part of his time chasing loose dogs. Even people who had no sympathy for dogs would go to the city council meetings and complain about how he was hounding the dogs to death.

Once my brother Barry saw this policeman moving along a cabin that belonged to an older woman whose son terrorized her when he drank. The cop jumped out of the corner of the cabin, pulled his gun, and yelled at the top of his lungs for the drunken son to put his hands in the air.

The son was badly shaken. Never had any of the Fort Yukon police used such a professional technique to arrest someone. The son was turned spread-eagle against the building, searched, handcuffed, read his rights, and led away to jail. After that incident he behaved himself for a long time.

I was willing to give the officer from L.A. the benefit of the doubt, but in time I found his racist talk to be unbearable, so I quit hoping that the city knew what it was doing when it hired him.

CHAPTER SEVENTEEN
Going to Oregon

186 / VELMA WALLIS

*N*ot long after I left my job as a police dispatcher, my youngest sister Becky traveled to Michigan, where she would live with our sister Clara and finish high school. I rented a small cabin to live in. When I wasn't there, I stayed at the Neegoogwandah cabin.

Barry and I spent hours talking about ways to better our lives. Although I was more of a talker and Barry was a doer, between the two of us we managed to dream up ideas to keep us busy.

Barry decided that I needed some kind of training. He was like that—always trying to get people to do things. One windy night I came down from Negoogwandah and found Barry all excited.

"Guess what?" he said.

I could not guess, so he told me what he had done. He had signed me up to attend a Job Corps school in Astoria, Oregon, a facility established to educate the dropouts of America. I was shocked.

"I don't want to go to that school!" I told him.

"But you can't live here in Fort Yukon forever," he said imploringly. "You have to move on."

"I don't want to, and you have no right to sign me up for something like that!" I said, determined not to go.

"But I already have it all set up, and your ticket and itinerary are right here," Barry said, holding out a packet to me.

I couldn't believe it. He had done all this without consulting me.

Barry was the one who tried to better my life. When he had money, he bought me clothes, shampoo, and books. I would not believe a word he said about my being special, but in my heart I thanked him. But I rejected all efforts to improve me, especially when his efforts came in such a highhanded manner.

At the end of the night, there was not much I could do but agree to get on the plane the next day.

"What about my things at Neegoogwandah?" I asked.

Barry said he would arrange for one of my brothers to pick up my belongings.

Suddenly, I was sharply aware of how threadbare my wardrobe was. I always dressed shabbily. That night Barry and I dug around in my mother's clothes and my sister's, trying to gather enough presentable clothing to send me away in.

Barry and I were close. When we were older, he was always trying to improve my life.

The next day, I waved goodbye to my family. I did not relish the feeling of being pushed out of my cocoon into an unknown world. I was not ready.

※ ※ ※

The Alaska Airlines flight to Seattle was uneventful. I had only to follow the itinerary. From there I flew to Portland, where I had to go to the Greyhound bus station.

When I arrived at the bus station, I could feel a change in the travelers' attitudes. At the airports everyone moved about busily, trying to make their connections, dressed as if in a fashion show. But here at the bus terminal, not only did people suddenly appear in shabby jeans and backpacks, but their attitudes matched their clothing. They became suspicious, silent, almost sullen, as they waited for their buses.

I copied the people at the bus station, keeping to myself, but I was lonely. I had spent months at our cabin alone and enjoyed every minute of my solitude. Here I was experiencing loneliness for the first time in a sea of people, and I felt alienated. The feeling assaulted my senses.

When I happened to make eye contact with someone, I smiled instantly and they quickly looked away. I gave up trying to be nice. I kept my eyes averted from others around me so that I could not see the blank looks on their faces.

The bus trip was uncomfortable. I could smell the latrine that passengers kept making trips to visit and the communal body odor generated by a large number of people crowding into a stifling vehicle. The nauseating smells made me want to throw up as the bus bounced to our destination.

The whole time I traveled from bus stop to bus stop, I cursed Barry for his impulsive ways. When I got out of this, I promised myself that I would have a long talk with him about minding his own business.

✳ ✳ ✳

The school was almost like a jail. I had been on my own too long to recognize authority. I felt that if I could survive out in the woods, I had earned the right to be treated like an adult. But the people who ran the school were teachers who had spent years teaching juvenile delinquents, and the kids I met there enlightened me more than I could have anticipated.

By then I was a twenty-year-old prude, and every day I was shocked by what I heard and saw. In the back of my mind, I was saying over and over, "Barry, I am going to kill you."

My roommates were three pretty girls who flaunted their sexuality wearing Frederick's of Hollywood outfits. Beside them I felt lacking. I had grown up with brothers and had not a feminine bone in my body. In my baggy jeans and hiking boots, I felt like a clumsy mess next to those girls who spent most of their time in front of the mirror.

My roommates were always chasing the young, rich students from the Middle East and Africa who attended a nearby university. These foreign students showered the young American girls with gifts of clothing and perfume. The girls spent much time boasting of their men. I listened earnestly, never having heard such talk before.

I had grown up watching men like my father use and abuse women like my mother, so I did not trust men. I was determined not to be like any of those abused women, but it was fun listening to these girls proudly describe how they attracted men.

As much as I enjoyed watching these young girls weave their spells, I could not find it in myself to participate. I gravitated toward a group of girls who did not drink, smoke, or chase boys. This was a safe route. We were here to learn.

Yet peer pressure was everywhere. I had never before felt this kind of seduction. It was in my room where the girls decorated themselves at night as they talked excitedly about their men, and it was in the bathrooms where women winked my way.

Once a young black woman patted my behind, and I was startled out of my senses.

"Don't ever touch me like that again," I said, shocked.

She shrugged and walked by nonchalantly. I felt violated.

A tall black man in one of my classes stared at me all the time. He said he was in love with me. I tried to ignore him. Later, he was taken to jail for raping a girl in one of the school bathrooms.

I noticed two girls who stood aside from all the action. I thought they were twins. They looked like the safe kind of people I wanted to befriend, so I made friendly overtures.

One day, I sat down at the bus stop and said "hello" to one of them. The other girl came storming up, took the first girl's hand, and dragged her away.

One of my acquaintances stood by, completely amused. When she saw how bewildered I was, my acquaintance explained that the two girls were "married." The jealous girl had thought that I was trying to steal her "wife." My face burned as my friend laughed at my naiveté.

I grew hungry for the company of people I could understand.

Even in the classroom there was pressure. One female teacher taught crafts. My friends and I all took her class because we were a lazy bunch and thought it would be easy.

In this class there was a pretty girl who looked like Valerie Bertinelli. Every day, whether it was hot or cold, she wore a mink coat, and she was always sarcastic in her dealings with us.

One day, the crafts teacher went on a long tirade, telling me how beautiful I was. I became the center of attention, and I found it thoroughly embarrassing. The girl in the mink coat smiled at me in amusement as I blushed.

After the teacher left, Ms. Mink Coat said, "Don't get too flattered there, girl. That woman's a lesbian. She says that to all the girls she's attracted to."

She watched my face fall. I was easy prey in those days, and it irritated me to no end.

* * *

I had chosen a telephone repair class. The first thing the instructor told me was that he hated it when girls thought they could do a man's job.

I would like to say that I stood my ground and made him believe I could do the job, but instead I was intimidated. When he made comments about the differences between a man's world and a woman's world, I could not speak up. I just kept my eyes down and wished I could be invisible while the guys in the class listened to the instructor's words. My upbringing had taught me to listen to this man and believe every word that he said about me.

I was depressed. I ate more and gained weight.

By then I had made friends with two Eskimo girls, Lana and Alene. Lana became a real friend; we just clicked, as friends do. Alene seemed too worldly for me, so I shied away from her although she was nice. In a couple weeks she decided that this school was not for her and she returned to Alaska. Then there was just Lana and me.

In Alaska, we would never have had contact because we lived on opposite sides of the country, but there in Astoria we came together like magnets. We learned about one another, but we were young and foolish, and mostly we felt like bores and wanted to be part of the school's social life. Everyone else seemed to be having fun.

I always thought of myself as being above peer pressure, but I was caving in. I thought it was time I loosened up a little and stopped taking life so seriously. This seemed to work for everyone else.

A bunch of teenage Vietnamese refugees were brought to the school. They tried to talk to Lana and me because we looked like them. Many times I was subjected to their outbursts, which sounded like the tongues of Babel. I listened and nodded my head. I felt they were telling me about their long boat trip from their country, where there had been nothing but turmoil. I figured they needed a sympathetic ear even if I couldn't understand their lanquage.

One time, when a bunch of us had spent the day in town, we waited for the bus that would take us back to the school. One of the Vietnamese men lay down in the street amid the heavy traffic. He knew the drivers would not run him over. It was a heady experience for him because he, and many like him, had faced death in their own country. The drivers stuck their heads out the windows and cursed him, but they made no move to get out of their cars and haul him off the pavement. The locals did not like us. They could barely conceal their prejudices.

Lana and I got stoned while waiting for the bus. A young Navajo girl stumbled in drunk and lay down on the floor, masturbating. My friend and I laughed at this. I felt sorry for the girl, but my mind was under the influence of drugs and everyone seemed so funny.

One of the counselors took the girl away. There must have been about thirty of us watching her. His sober ears heard our giggles, and he began to shout at us.

* * *

Another time Lana and I went to the local liquor store and bought a pint of whiskey. We planned to get stinking drunk.

The man behind the counter questioned our age. Although we did not have identification, he sold us the bottle.

On the way back to school, we nervously debated which of us would carry the bottle past the guarded fence. Finally, as we drew near, we decided I would do it. I started to tremble.

When I got off the bus, guilt must have been written all over my face. One of the guards took one look at me and asked me to come inside his little office. Lana walked away without a backwards glance.

"I'm disappointed in you," the guard said. The guards saw us every day and often bantered with us. I hung my head in shame for letting him down. Never mind about letting myself down.

"I thought you were one of the kids who would succeed here," the guard went on. I listened, unable to utter a response, for my guilt held me silent.

The school counselors said that next day I would appear before my peers, and they would decide my fate.

I felt foolish. First of all, kids younger than I were drinking day and night. Back in Fort Yukon, many kids were alcoholics, and we were considered old and used up by the time we were twenty. Yet here I was, about to be chastised like a child. I could not see past the impending shame of being disciplined before my peers—not for trying to drink but for getting caught.

Most of all, I could not bear the shame of facing my friends, the guards, the counselors, and seeing their disappointment. They had more faith in me than I had in myself. All I had wanted was to get drunk and have fun and friends. Because of that, I was going to be punished. The shame was more than I could bear.

CHAPTER EIGHTEEN
Back to Fort Yukon

*T*hat night, Lana and I plotted a way out of the whole mess. We were both over eighteen and felt we were our own people.

"Let's just walk out of here," I said.

The idea took hold, and we packed our belongings.

The guards saw us go but had no right to stop us. I remember the look in their eyes. If I had a father who cared about me, I imagine that was how he would have looked as I walked away from the school toward the dark highway.

We hitchhiked north that night. We knew it was dangerous, but we were young and foolish, and danger was what drove us on.

We were lucky to survive, for that spring of 1980 serial killers were out and about in the Pacific Northwest. All sorts of people picked us up—mostly men but also women. We kept our senses sharp, ready to fight off any serial killers we might encounter.

As afraid as we were of meeting a predator, the drivers in the cars often were afraid of us. Many would shake their heads at us, either apologetically or in reprimand. Once we got a ride by hiding all of our bags behind one suitcase to make it look like we did not have a lot of luggage. The man who picked us up cursed us for our deception, but gave us a ride anyway.

Mount St. Helens had just erupted, and the area from Astoria to Seattle was covered in ash. I can't imagine what we must have looked like but I knew that ash was dusting my hair, my face, my boots, and my teeth. Frequently we were in desperate need of a bath. Once we sponged ourselves clean in a McDonald's restroom.

✳ ✳ ✳

When we made it to Seattle, my friend called her cousin, who had lived there for twenty years. He was a good person but he loved to drink. Even with a wonderful wife and two beautiful children, he still slunk off to Fourth Avenue to drink.

A couple of times he took us downtown. He tried to get us to drink, but Lana knew her cousin well and told me to beware. When he tried to introduce us to his cronies, Lana scowled at him, for she saw no point in getting to know his friends. We were in his hands, and when he tried to get us to party, Lana would have none of it. She had had enough of trouble, and she wanted us to stay safe as we tried to find a way back to Alaska.

Lana's cousin's wife was a sweet woman who helped us get jobs at the Goodwill store. I was in good company as I sorted clothes and was promoted according to my work ethics. The woman who sat nearest me on this assembly line smelled of whiskey and complained endlessly about her life and her problems. She drove me to distraction.

I saw how the people at the Goodwill store cared for people who needed a helping hand. But I also saw that the people who needed a helping hand were used to getting this kind of help, and therefore they would not help themselves.

Every day my friend and I walked a couple miles to work. After two weeks, we were sorely disappointed in our paychecks. We had a lot of expenses and knew it would take more than a couple of months to raise the money to get home. After receiving a second little paycheck I called home. Barry gathered enough money for me to come home. Lana's family helped with her airfare too. Our life in the big city was not meant to be.

✳ ✳ ✳

It was late June when I got off the plane in Fairbanks. The air was clean and fragrant in a way I had never noticed before, and the people were tanned and healthy-looking. I came back to Alaska able to appreciate things I had taken for granted.

Returning to Fort Yukon, I understood for the first time how isolated I had been during my time away, and I appreciated the few people who welcomed me back. Despite all the drinking that went on, the people here were just simple souls striving to live a peaceful existence within their comfort zone. They were friendly people, and I could understand them.

My mom was still drinking, and she ranted and raved at me for going AWOL. I told her that I had not been AWOL but missing in action.

For years to come I would fill Barry's ear with tales of the trip to Astoria. He swore he was sorry that he had ever sent me because it meant he had to hear the stories over and over.

That didn't stop him from meddling in my life. Years later, without our permission, he arranged for my sister Becky and me to work in the canneries in Valdez. Of course we went along with it until we realized it was not our mission in life to process fish. At least that job was good exercise. To anyone who wants to get into good shape, I recommend getting a job in fish processing rather than joining a weight-loss program.

∗ ∗ ∗

My mother continued to struggle with her drinking. After all our years of effort and throwing tantrums, one day she was alone and found herself looking in the mirror. She saw her reflection and knew then that she did not want to die in that condition. She made up her mind to change.

It was hard for her to quit. Many times we would hear her old line—that she was going uptown and would be right back. In past years we had let her walk out the door, glad that she was going to be gone for a while; living with a person who wants to drink is nerve-racking. But now we knew our mother wanted to do better, so we chased after her. One of us would go for a long walk with her while she struggled desperately with her addiction.

As days passed and she managed to stay sober, Mom applied for a janitorial position at an office building. She got the job. She worked for more than five years before the years of neglecting her body began to take their toll on her health.

Just as a war always has an aftermath, years of addiction are followed by an aftermath too. When Mom sobered up, she found that her offspring were still living with her as if they were children. If we weren't living in her house, we still went to her house and spent all of our spare time with her. We were like little children, afraid to be without our mother.

"One day you were children and the next thing I know, everyone is grown up," she said once. "I ask myself, when did this happen?"

It was hard for us to cut ourselves free from our mother's apron strings. Where she had been drunk and oblivious to the fact that we had grown up, we had been sober and oblivious to the fact that we needed to grow up.

Children of alcoholics are stunted mentally, emotionally, and spiritually along with the addicted person. We thought that Mom was the one with the problem. But after she sobered up, we had to begin the same process of gaining sobriety. We discovered that there was no more room for sickness or unhealthy thoughts. We were like Neegoogwandah when it had been ravaged by fire back in 1968. Now we had to start the long, slow process of healing.

Just because we could see we had been stuck in limbo does not mean that we could readily divorce ourselves from it all and move on into the proverbial sunset.

For my family, that journey has taken years. Some of my siblings have not yet begun their healing process. On the journey, we have often run into seemingly insurmountable mountains and uncrossable rivers, and disasters still occur that threaten to destroy the remaining structure of our family.

CHAPTER NINETEEN

Barry

*T*he disaster that most threatened us came through Barry.

Barry was the smartest, the most lovable, and the one most likely to succeed. By having hope in the world around him, he gave hope to everyone he came in contact with.

As the Administrator for the Native Village of Fort Yukon, he came up with inventive ways to improve village life. On the one side he rolled up his sleeves and wrote grant applications, and on the other side he allowed himself to dream—but not too much, for he knew that dreams are okay but hard work is what will improve the world around us.

One of his favorite dreams was to organize all the villages to boycott shopping in Anchorage and Fairbanks. Politicians often threatened to cut funding to the villages, which they said drained the state's coffers. Barry wanted to show the two cities how much they depended on the villages for their survival.

Barry was starting to understand the mechanics of politics, and he enjoyed finding ways to one-up the opposition. I didn't understand politics, but I would listen as he told me of these things. One of them was working with all the villages to organize Native voters and elect a governor of our choice. He also tried to get all the surrounding lands that belonged to our local corporation into tribal hands as a protection against financial failures. Barry worked toward countless other goals, but he did not want any public acknowledgment of his efforts, for that was not his way.

Deep down he wanted to start things moving and then have better leaders take over for him, so he could eventually pick up his paints and palette and create some art. He had always dabbled. When we were younger and poorer, he helped buy food with his paintings. Some in the village knew his work and were willing to pay a hundred dollars for a painting of a local landmark. Barry was a big fan of Andrew Wyeth and later, Jamie Wyeth, and wanted to do real art. Yet life called him, and there was much work to be done in Fort Yukon, so regretfully he put aside his artistic desire and worked.

Barry had friendships with people from all walks of life. He never judged people and he detested those who did. Once, Barry jokingly said that had I not been his sister we would have had nothing in common. I felt lucky to be his sister, for without him I would not have known the better part of myself.

Barry and I were thrown together through circumstance. To begin with, we were dreamers. We shared a kind of vague dream that perhaps all this chaos around us was not necessary, and that our future life could be less chaotic. We dreamed of having a good house and getting a good education in a place with no liquor store—the source of all our miseries.

Like our father, we were not religious. We detested religious people who tried to shove their beliefs down our throats. We were all for spiritual values, but we had had enough of guilt and demons. We didn't want to hear doomsday preached.

As a result, we remained in between the saints and the sinners. That was a fine line to walk. It made for a lonely life in our village.

In our early twenties, Barry and I wanted to make Fort Yukon a better place for those who did not have fathers to chart a path for them. We wanted to make it easier for children of alcoholics to survive. There were always fly-by-night programs that tried to do just that, but when the money ran out, the workers dispersed.

I was a talker, apt to sit around draining your teapot and your hospitality, while Barry was more inclined to roll up his sleeves and go to work. He hated my dreaming ways and wanted me to get on with it. His favorite saying was "Velma, either poop or get off the pot."

When I wrote down the story that my mother had told me about the two old women, it was in a rough draft. Barry did not care. He was so thrilled that he passed the story around. He wanted it published. I just wanted people to hear the story.

When I was about to forget about the story and start on one of my many other schemes and dreams, Barry would get me back on track, telling me to try to get the story published. In my heart, I could not imagine myself as a published writer. My self-esteem just wasn't there. But Barry made copies of the story and tried to bring it to people's attention.

People in Fort Yukon liked the story, but once they read it they never said anything more about it. I would shrug and move on, but Barry would dig the story up time and again. Finally he and his friend and cousin, Marilyn Savage, sent me in the direction of Lael Morgan at the University of Alaska Fairbanks. Meeting Lael eventually lead to the story being published as the book *Two Old Women*.

When *Two Old Women* became an instant success and won the Western States Book Award, I was taken completely by surprise. Barry, on the other hand, smiled in a way that told me that he had always known it would.

After the fanfare, I decided I had had enough of success. Barry laughed.

"You can't turn around now," he said. "You were meant to tell stories in writing."

So I began working on my second story. I sent him the first draft while I was on a road trip. My mother, who watched him open the package, complained, "Where's my copy? I'm the one who told her those stories!"

✳ ✳ ✳

Barry was determined to make a difference on this earth. I was too. But he was of a different caliber than I was. When I attended the University of Alaska Fairbanks, I set myself up for failure there, but when Barry enrolled he enjoyed it to the fullest. It challenged his intellect. After a couple years of school, he lost interest in sitting in classes and listening to lectures while there were so many things yet to be done in the village, so he came home.

While Barry worked hard on his dreams, I continued to dream plans in my head. In time that would begin to separate us. Barry had learned that if a dream was to be accomplished, you had to step outside your head and buckle down for the hard work. I always felt that because of my lack of schooling I was not fit to learn any more. But Barry saw that as just an excuse and told me so many times.

As Barry worked furiously to build our town, I dreamed of a Utopian society. At one point I moved to the Venetie Reservation, thinking that would be the place where Indians were what my ideals told me they should be: sober, self-sufficient, and healthy.

Barry called it my geographical change. He repeated to me that you may think you can leave a problem behind, but actually you take it with you. Other times he would say, "Velma, if you are not part of the solution, then you are part of the problem." He loved those one-sentence truisms, and in that way he reminded me of my father.

Needless to say, I had a rude awakening that Utopian societies are only dreams created by those who are not able to face reality. I had to face the fact that if addictions existed in Fort Yukon, then they probably existed in the surrounding villages as well. I wanted to run from it all, but Barry stayed, enjoying his life doing what he dreamed—making his home village a better place to live.

Each time I left Fort Yukon, I left because I got tired of seeing people drunk. I hated to see pregnant women staggering down the road. I hated that each year a whole new flock of young ones picked up the bottle.

Most of all I hated that we Gwich'in were straying from our tradition of caring and knowing one another. I was bitter that alcohol had created chasms. Each time we awoke from a drunken brawl, we compromised one more aspect of ourselves. Each time we freely gave ourselves over to our addictions, we were less Gwich'in.

I ran from it, but I grew to admire Barry for staying. Many times I patted Barry on the back for having the courage to stay and work on these problems with such dedication.

Once I told him that he and I were like the last of the Mohicans; we were the only ones of our age who hadn't succumbed to alcohol and died from it.

When I said this, Barry squirmed and gave me one of his guilty laughs. He never let on once that he was about to abandon ship.

When Barry died I looked far back into our past and realized that we all are in danger of losing the fight to survive. I had thought that because we refrained from drinking we were safe. I did not consider how the effects of growing up in a dysfunctional environment could set you up for some kind of unexpected failure.

✷ ✷ ✷

Barry's one flaw, and the precursor to his death, was a trait that most of us share to a lesser or a greater degree: procrastination, which is the child of denial. In all his efforts to save Fort Yukon from itself, he had not been able to save himself from himself, and in that time he contracted HIV.

Barry was thirty-five when he died. We always knew that he would never marry. But some part of us wanted to believe that he was not

Barry died at the age of 35. I felt abandoned and angry.

already locked into his sexual preferences. I suppose it is like that with families when they discover that one of them will not conform to society's strict codes of behavior. We wanted to bypass this issue simply because it was not a comfortable subject.

Since we were small, my father forbade us to mention sex, always referring to it as "dirty." So when we became teenagers, Barry told me that he and I could talk about anything under the sun except sex.

When I questioned him about whether he would take a mate, he would bluntly say "No!"—end of discussion. As we matured, this was in the back of my mind, but I made allowances for my brothers. We did not have the type of upbringing that encouraged intimacy.

Barry kept his private life off-limits, and when he became sick, he told no one. In retrospect, he must have wanted to tell us his secret, but he must have felt that he could not trust anyone. He went through his pain, sorrow, and realization alone, for his time of letting go was beginning.

Of all the problems we might have suspected, we never guessed this dreadful disease. But we saw many signs of him becoming a person who had given up—this he was not able to hide.

Once, when some hoodlums broke into his house and wrote graffiti all over it, Barry simply moved into my mother's house. We helped him fix up his house, but he seemed not to care.

In local politics, he stopped fighting against those who wanted to take over his position. I was angry and rallied for him, but Barry just told me to behave myself.

We had been raised on my father's non-belief. My father swore he was an atheist, but deep down we knew he was an agnostic. Religion had scarred us, and we trusted no one. Toward the end of his life, I believe Barry looked beyond our reality. He asked questions of those he respected, and he changed as a person. He was at peace with himself.

That drove me crazy. I wanted him to be the fighter he had always been. He had been my leader—telling me how to act, how to dress, and how to think. All of a sudden, when I asked for his advice, he began telling me to decide things for myself.

I felt abandoned, and I reacted in anger. To heck with you, I thought to myself. I decided to do things on my own. On my last book tour before he died, I made up my mind to tell him that I would no longer depend on him to be my mentor. I had no idea that this was exactly what he wanted.

✳ ✳ ✳

Long before Barry died, he told us that he had heard the owl call his name. He showed us a snowy white owl that hung around his house. He told me stories of leaving his body one night. It frightened him when he had floated to the ceiling. He looked down and saw his body, and pushed himself back down. Later, he heard chanting of ancestors from long ago. He seemed more interested in exploring the wonders of nature than in participating in politics.

In the fall before he died, I was ranting about a local political event as we walked, and Barry seemed to listen.

"Did you ever notice that the leaves turn yellow overnight?" he asked, distracting me from my train of thought. I was thrown off balance, but I was trying to understand the new Barry. I said I hadn't noticed.

"Just yesterday the leaves were green, and today they are yellow," he said with wonder in his eyes.

I could only say "Hmm," as I frowned at him. He had definitely changed!

I felt something was amiss, yet I could not put my finger on it. It was almost as if my observant self had been put to sleep so that I remained blind to what was happening. I believe that Barry knew this, and in some mysterious way he kept the shroud over my eyes.

Many times I would ask him to tell me what was going on with him, and he would shrug and tell me all was well. I wanted to believe him, so I did.

I think that Barry allowed us to bypass all the things he knew we would feel if he told us his situation. He was like that. Always trying to spare people the trouble. He would carry his burden without any help.

Fate had a different ending reserved for him. When Barry tried to die in Fort Yukon, concerned people forced him into the hospital. There he faced us all, though he could never talk, for he had too many tubes in him. Any one of us standing around his bed would have given our life for him.

* * *

I was on an author tour when Barry was taken to the hospital. He had gotten intensely sick, but until the last minute resisted help. I could go into many details about Barry's passing on, but it is truly a personal matter. I will say that when the doctor asked me uncomfortable personal questions about my brother, I tried to explain everything about Barry, from how he got the imprint of a zipper under his right eye to events of the day he was born. I wanted to protect him from the judgment of the world.

When we began to prepare for my brother's death, I sat in the waiting room of the ICU. A television was on. A commercial came on, and to this day I have never seen it again. The commercial said that there are three things that do not care who you are or how rich you are; they do not choose you because of your status in life or any other category you fall into. These three things are Ebola, E. Coli, and the

AIDS virus. So began our three long weeks of watching a beloved brother leave our world.

Our lives had been steeped in superstitions, ignorance, addictions, and sorrow. Barry's death made me realize that we are products of our beliefs. Only through deep concentration and focus can we change ourselves for the better, and even then we can change only a little.

My family came together from all parts of the country. Together we held Barry's hands and wept. He had been the honorable one, and now he was being taken by a dreaded and agonizing death. We were numbed to the core.

I thought Barry's death would shatter us forever, but when he died, we held his hands as he went quietly to sleep. There was a deep sense of peace that filled us all, despite the fact that we were losing the one member of the family whom we never wanted to lose.

As Clara held his hand, I cried out his name, suddenly realizing this dream was for real. Barry opened his eyes as if I had called him back from death.

"It's okay, Barry, we'll all take care of one another," Clara said. She squeezed his hands, and he nodded and went to sleep.

Outside the windows of the ICU, a flock of ravens spread out into a shape of a V, darkening the otherwise bright November sky.

Epilogue

Once, when I took my Aunt Nina to midnight mass at our church on New Year's night, she began to cry.

"What's the matter, Auntie?" I asked.

She said she missed all the people from the past. She said she did not know any of us younger ones, and things were not the same.

That night she staggered home in tears, leaving me standing there. I was seventeen and in the darkness I felt abandoned. I wanted to call out to her, "I'm here!" but as much as she did not understand my generation, I did not understand hers.

In 1992, when *Two Old Women* was published, some in our community believed that our legends should not be told to the world. At a small gathering in Fort Yukon, an old man stood up and said, "What Velma is doing is good. It's about time our stories are told. They should have been told before the elders died fifty years ago." That man understood that our stories, the memories of our people, are the things left to hold us together.

In Harold Napoleon's paper *Yuuyaraq: The Way of the Human Being*, he said that in the time of transition Native people experienced tremendous loss of culture and storytelling. In the time of the devastating epidemics, which Napoleon called "The Great Deaths," people stopped talking about themselves and their history. The people who succumbed to the deaths took with them important details that were lost forever. All that remained were the few and fragmented tidbits of stories that still were being told here and there. As a result, our culture has become diluted by other value systems that go completely against the things our ancestors believed.

Each year we lose elders who understood the past and spoke our Native language. I fear that our young ones will never know the beauty of life that existed once upon a time, before the coming of drinking and drugs.

Then I remind myself that I, too, am a product of alcoholism. I've come to the realization that stories must be preserved for our children so they will not think what they are experiencing in their villages is all that has ever been. I almost believed that drinking and drugs were all we as Native people had ever been about until that day when my mother first told me the story about the two old women. Then I saw clearly that we were once strong and grounded, with a long history of survival. I saw hope that we could still be the people we once were, not in the literal sense, but possessing the same pride that our ancestors had before the epidemics and cultural changes.

A few things still hold us back. One is an idea that early missionaries and teachers drilled into our parents' minds—and our minds also—that it is not good to be who we are: Gwich'ins, Tlingets, Haida, Eyak, Aleut, Eskimos, or whatever other tribe we are. A subconscious part of us still believes it is better to be a cowboy than an Indian.

When my publisher, Lael Morgan, sought moral support from regional Native agencies in Fairbanks for *Two Old Women,* the leaders did not want any association with the story and its reminder of barbaric practices from their past. They did not want the world to know of the survival techniques our ancestors used because they conflicted with the new values that have been drilled into our minds for almost a hundred years. New ways of thinking were forced on us through humiliation and fear. The effects still are being felt by the indigenous people of today, preventing them from being proud of who they have been as a people.

The second thing that holds us back from being healed and being healthy is our reluctance to move into the future with a healthy balance of the old while we live in the new. I always hear Native speakers say—and I have used this rhetoric myself—that we have a foot in each culture. It's almost as if we still fear that missionaries and teachers will return to slap our hands and our mouths if we dare to reclaim our past.

Like victims of abuse, we must acknowledge that we *are* proud of our past and want to own some of our past values, as opposed to the values that were given to us. There is nothing wrong with that. We must dispense with the feelings of shame for wanting to be Indians instead of cowboys. When we were growing up, one of my sisters had a doll that had blue eyes. That sister swore she would have children with blue eyes, and she did. I saw nothing wrong with being Indian, or Native, and I try to teach my children that today.

One last thing that holds back our healing as people is an unhealthy sense of nostalgia. For me, this is the memory of my aunt, of Itchoo, and of my father, and the past way of life I was privi leged to glimpse. It is with great effort that I pull myself back into the present, for I cannot abandon my children.

Like an alcoholic, I take one day at a time. I teach myself to look into the future and not yearn for the past and its people; to honor them through their stories but not to fall into nostalgia which caused so many people to sink into depression. After Barry's death, I felt a powerful pull to disappear into depression and defeat, but my children kept calling me back.

Author's Afterword

My story is not unique—not within my culture or within other cultures. Out there are people whose lives have been affected by alcohol in far more devastating ways. But in sharing this story, I am working toward reconciliation. I hope to move on, for the sake of my children's future, and for mine. I wanted to chronicle the lives of those whose lives went by too quickly. There were too many of them, and they each had their own story about a life interrupted by this very subtle disease called alcoholism.

Two people once asked me different questions about Native people.

One was, "Why don't you Native people forget the past and move on?"

The other question was, "Why can't you Native people drink normally like us white people?"

Both questions left me dumbfounded. If only it were that easy!

I will say that as Alaska's Native people—Athabascans, Eskimos, Aleuts, Tlingets, Yupiks, and Haida—we cannot simply wipe clean the slate of our recent history of alcoholism, child abuse, domestic violence, murder, rape, fetal alcohol syndrome, drug abuse, ignorance, and dependency.

Yet we are a smart people who have lived a resourceful existence for thousands of years. We will learn to heal and adjust. Then, like our ancestors, we will be able to move onward in search of our next good hunting ground.

About the Author

Velma Wallis, one of Alaska's best-known authors, was one of thirteen children. When she was thirteen, her father died and she left school to help her mother raise her younger siblings. Years later, she moved to her family's traditional hunting land, a twelve-mile walk from the village, and learned the traditional survival skills of hunting and trapping. An avid reader, she passed her high school literacy equivalency exam and began her first literary project—writting down a legend her mother had told her, about two abandoned old women and their struggle to survive.

Wallis won the 1993 Western States Book Award and a 1994 Pacific Northwest Booksellers Award for her first book, *Two Old Women*, which has been translated into seventeen languages and is a bestseller in Germany, The Netherlands, and Spain.

Recommendations

for readers seeking a greater understanding of Alaska and its Native people:

ART & ESKIMO POWER
The Life and Times of Alaskan Howard Rock
Lael Morgan, paperback, $16.95

BIRD GIRL & THE MAN WHO FOLLOWED THE SUN
An Athabascan Indian Legend from Alaska
Velma Wallis, hardbound, $19.95

COLD RIVER SPIRITS
The Legacy of an Athabascan-Irish Family from Alaska
Jan Harper-Haines, hardbound, $19.95

ON THE EDGE OF NOWHERE
Jim Huntington & Lawrence Elliott, paperback, $14.95

SEVEN WORDS FOR WIND
Essays and Field Notes from Alaska's Pribilof Islands
Sumner MacLeish, hardbound, $16.95

SPIRIT OF THE WIND
The Story of Alaska's George Attla, Legendary Sled Dog Sprint Champ
Lew Freedman, paperback, $14.95

TWO OLD WOMEN
An Alaska Legend of Betrayal, Courage, and Survival
Velma Wallis, hardbound, $16.95

These titles can be found or special-ordered at your local bookstore. A wide assortment of Alaska books also can be ordered at the publisher's website, www.EpicenterPress.com or by calling 1-800-950-6663.